Title I

COOL, HOT AND BLUE

CHARLES BOECKMAN

Cool, Hot and Blue

A HISTORY OF JAZZ FOR YOUNG PEOPLE

ROBERT B. LUCE, INC. / Washington, D. C.

COOL, HOT AND BLUE

Library of Congress Catalog Card Number: 68–21535

Manufactured in the United States of America
Kingsport Press, Inc.
Kingsport, Tennessee

To my brother Roy, my sister Lola
and my wife Patti, who share
my enthusiasm for and enjoyment of music.

"The story of jazz should be in all the schools, so the children would know where their music comes from."

——*Hear Me Talkin' to Ya*

FOREWORD

This book is intended to be an introduction to the world, people and sounds of jazz music. We regret that we have to pass so many great contributors to the jazz field with no more than a nod, and in some cases, not even that—but to meet them all would require a much thicker book. To every name we have omitted, we offer our regrets. However, since their music is around to speak with more eloquence than our printed words, we know the lover of jazz will soon meet them.

CONTENTS

CHAPTER 1

THE IMPORTANCE OF JAZZ

Music is the most intensely personal form of art we have. Nearly all of us are in touch with music in our daily lives. We awaken to music from clock radios, listen to the latest hit songs while driving to school and hear background melodies in many of the stores where we shop. When we see a movie the story is dramatized by an appropriate musical score. Music is part of our football games, pep rallies, television programs and church services. For most of us, it has a deeply moving, emotional meaning. It can put us in a romantic mood, or make us gay or sad, or set our feet to tapping.

Generally speaking, music can be divided into two groups: serious and popular. Serious music includes symphonies, operas, concertos, chamber music, formal church programs—in short, all the forms of classical music, both old and modern, given to us by gifted composers and performed by skilled musicians singly and in groups.

Popular music in its many forms—ballads, rock 'n' roll, dance music, hit songs—has deep roots in American jazz, with the exception of those folk songs which predate it. Jazz is a great American contribution to world culture. Other art forms were handed down to us from Europe and Asia, but jazz music was born in our country. It is a unique form of expression and it has made a great musical impact on the rest of the world. American jazz in its many forms is played and enjoyed the world over, from Japan to Italy, to Russia, to South America. The great jazz musicians of America are welcomed like visiting heros when they perform abroad.

Jazz is so important to the cultural image of the United States, that our State Department sponsors worldwide tours by American performers. Such well-known artists as Duke Ellington, Louis Armstrong, Dizzy Gillespie and Jack Teagarden have played their own personal kind of jazz all the way from South Africa to Moscow. They give command performances before kings and queens. Louis Armstrong, on one of his tours, had an audience with the Pope in the Vatican. When Benny Goodman and his orchestra performed in Russia in the summer of 1962, he received an overwhelming ovation. His concert in Moscow was attended by important members of the Russian government, including premier Nikita Khrushchev. Our jazz trumpet player and singer Louis Armstrong is so beloved all over the world, that he has been nicknamed "Ambassador Satch." Truly, American jazz musicians have been ambassadors of good will, bridging gaps of language and customs and political differences, creating friendly relations and understanding where formal statesmen have sometimes failed.

Jazz music has not always been as acceptable as it is today. A relatively few years ago, many people thought it not entirely respectable—not the sort of thing nice people listened to. One of the reasons for this early rejection was jazz was first heard in honky-tonks and districts of bad reputation. It has come a long way since those days, all the way to the respectability of concert halls. Specialized jazz music has even been composed for church services.

We are in a unique and lucky position in regard to jazz. Because it has developed largely since the start of this century, many of the jazz pioneers are still alive and performing today. To compare it to classical music, it is as if we were living in an age when Beethoven, Brahms, Haydn and Tchaikovsky were all active and finding new ways to express their musical ideas. Also, the invention of the phonograph when jazz music was emerging as a definite form has given us another unique advantage: nearly all the great jazz performers, living and dead, have left us priceless recordings of their performances.

Being able to hear the individual performer, or the performances of certain groups or orchestras, is especially important in jazz music. In classical music, the composer writes all his musical ideas in notes on his scores, so we can fairly well duplicate what he wanted us to hear even though he may have died two hundred years ago. Jazz music, however, is a more spontaneous and individualistic form of expression, created on the spot. A performance would be lost forever if it were not for the modern miracles of the phonograph and tape recorder.

It is easy to see evidence of worldwide acceptance of jazz music and its importance to our own culture. But when we try to define jazz, we run into difficulty. It is a rapidly developing art form that it has branched into different schools or types of music. One kind might sound quite different from another, yet both would be considered jazz.

To one person, jazz music means a group of young musicians wearing long hair who, with amplified guitars, are playing a window-shaking version of the latest rock 'n' roll hit. To others, jazz is a Dixieland band playing on Bourbon Street in New Orleans, or a rousing big-band arrangement by Count Basie, a recording by clarinetist Pete Fountain, a melody sung by Ella Fitzgerald, a folk song by Peter, Paul and Mary or a way-out progressive jazz solo by Miles Davis.

Some attempts have been made to put labels on the various forms of jazz: Traditional New Orleans Jazz, Chicago Style, West Coast Jazz, Bebop, Mainstream and Progressive.

But which of these really is jazz? It's a bit confusing. In the broadest sense, they are all forms of jazz or grew out of jazz. Jazz music covers more than just one style. It is more than *just* popular music, though jazz is popular music. It is a distinctive art form that owes much of its popularity to the way it can communicate the human emotions we all understand, and to the way it appeals to a basic love of rhythm which seems instinctive in most humans.

The greatest jazz performers seem least able to explain what they are doing. When asked to explain jazz or swing, Ella Fitzgerald once said, "Why, er—swing is—well, you sort of feel—uh—uh—I don't know—you just swing!"

During an interview on the "Bell Telephone Hour" program about jazz in the spring of 1967, Pete Fountain expounded:

> "There's a feeling—it's hard to explain. You just feel it . . . it just projects and I think the people can feel it when it's working . . . When it clicks out there, they just lean back and they can be talking, but they keep quiet for a while . . . Then you know it's working . . . then you know you have them and they have you—It's the same thing. You sell 'em part of you, part of yourself way down—no, not selling, you're *giving* . . ."

Perhaps Fats Waller, as quoted in *The Story of Jazz,* gave the most succinct reply to the question. When a nice old lady asked him, "What is jazz, Mr. Waller?" the legendary Fats sighed, "Madam, if you don't know by now, DON'T MESS WITH IT!"

Despite Mr. Waller's admonition, we are going to "mess with it." Because through a bit of understanding one can learn to appreciate jazz music and have some knowledge about what the jazz performer is doing.

The best way to start to understand and appreciate jazz is to learn a little about how this music happened to be born in America. If we understand the influences that gave birth to jazz music, we'll be in a much better position to know what we are listening to. And as we trace the growth of jazz from its beginnings, we'll see how it branched as it developed.

The history of jazz is colorful and entertaining. It is peopled with strong personalities and linked with the changing events and social patterns in the United States. In each decade it has reflected the temperament of the times—the ragtime piano of the Gay Nineties, the rousing war songs of 1917, the Chicago Style jazz of the Roaring Twenties, the big-band swing of the depression years, the cool jazz of the fifties and the big beat of the sixties. Jazz has spanned an era from the Mississippi riverboats to the supersonic jet age.

CHAPTER 2

WHERE DID IT BEGIN?

It was late at night and the swinging beat of jazz music floated into the narrow streets of the French Quarter of New Orleans. In a smoky, crowded room, an old trumpet player raised his battered horn to his lips. It fit his hands well. For more than fifty years he had been holding a horn like this.

There had been times when he'd gotten away from music. The times, half-forgotten now, when he'd worked on the railroad and when he'd picked cotton—hard times when nobody seemed to want to pay to hear him play and a man had to eat. But he had always come back to music. It still had a hold on him after all these years. The rhythm had a way of getting to him, and the excitement was still there, a little faded perhaps, but still there.

He could feel the throb of the drumbeat reaching deep inside, carrying him along, and the chords of the piano making harmonies echo in his mind, beautiful sounds. He played from his heart, the way he'd always played, the only way he knew. The tones spilled from his horn like golden butter, melting in the warmth of his music. There was emotion in his playing, a touch of sadness about the things a man has to endure in life, but a burst of joy at the good times, too.

He was playing jazz.

Later, after the horn was packed away in a case even more battered than the instrument and tucked under his arm, he left the place and walked along the dark streets in the early morning mist. He had seen many lonely streets in many cities in these quiet, early morning hours. It was part of the life of a jazz man.

He walked until he came to the river, the big old muddy Mississippi, and he paused for a moment to rest on the levee on his way home. Tonight his mind was filled with memories, a sign of growing old, he supposed. He was thinking about all the music he'd heard in his life and all the great jazz musicians he'd known and admired: Bunny Berigan, Jack Teagarden, Bix Beiderbecke—they'd blown their mighty horns for a while and now they were gone while their music lingered like eddies in the muddy river current below.

He thought about this old city where he'd been born. He remembered when his mother had taken him to revival meetings, the handclapping rhythm of the hymn singing, where he first learned how rhythm could make people sway, how it could stir their hearts. He remembered following the brass bands home from funerals and how the people danced in the street behind them. Once he'd heard the great King Oliver playing his trumpet in a marching band. He remembered, back in his faraway childhood, how once he'd stood outside a honky-tonk in Storyville and listened to Jelly Roll Morton playing piano like no other living man. That had been way back before World War I, a long, long time ago.

The years rolled by in his memory, the twenties when he'd played his own horn in speakeasies owned by gangsters, the lean depression years of the thirties when he'd gotten away from music for a while, then came back to it when he got a job in a big band. They'd started calling the music swing then, but underneath it was still the same he remembered hearing as a child, the mixture of rhythmic church music, marching bands and honky-tonk piano. Then came the forties and a younger generation of jazz musicians who played a new kind of jazz that sounded strange and complicated to his ears. Now, in the sixties the rock 'n' roll popular music took him back again to the rhythm and blues he'd heard as a child.

And he was back in the city where he was born, still playing his horn in the time that was left . . .

When and how did it all begin—this music that has such a hold on the heart of America and the world? Who invented jazz? Where was it first played?

To the best of our knowledge what we now call traditional New Orleans style jazz was first heard around the turn of this century. Some say New Orleans was the birthplace and it spread from there to other parts of the country, while other music historians believe that jazz began spontaneously in different parts of the country. We know that jazz grew from a number of sources—religious music, early American folk music, music of minstrel shows, the songs and dances of Negro slaves, ragtime piano and the marching brass bands. These last two are most closely related to early jazz; and traditional New Orleans jazz is only a step away from march music.

The American Negro made a great contribution to the emotional, freewheeling, strongly rhythmic kind of folk music that developed into jazz. As slaves from Africa, they brought a powerful sense of rhythm and dance. Once in the New World, they absorbed the European musical traditions of harmony and form, and conveniently fitted together the African and European musical ideas. The result was an Afro-American style of music all their own. Since the African was used to a different musical scale, he tried to adjust his musical ear to the European scale by adding a blues-y kind of note that could sound low-down and haunting.

Jazz music was a social phenomenon that grew out of many things that were happening in the United States in the 1800's. Plantations, field hands, camp meetings, frontier towns, steamboats, minstrel shows, brass bands, the Civil War and emancipation of the slaves, the Gay Nineties—they all played a part. We were going through a period when inventive genius and creative inspiration were bursting like a Fourth-of-July fireworks display on the American scene. The electric light, phonograph, automobile and airplane were all invented between 1875 and 1910. Was it just coincidental that jazz music took form during this same period? All of the things generated by the restless adolescence of a young nation needed to be expressed in a stirring, spontaneous kind of music, and that's what jazz was.

To the early jazzman, formal music was dead music, written for the most part by composers who were long gone, and rigidly performed according to the manner in which it had been written ten, twenty or a hundred years ago. But jazz was inventive, spontaneous music, composed by the performer as he played. And it was eloquent music, giving full range to the artist's expression beyond the limitation of words. It was a restless music well suited to the times and temperament of a young nation.

Above all, it was a highly individualistic form of music colored by the performer's personality and style. A Brahms symphony performed by a competent American orchestra might hardly be distinguishable, except to a highly trained musician, from the same work performed by a European group—the individual performers are submerged in the group. But a jazz clarinet solo played, for example, by Benny Goodman sounds very different from any other clarinet solo in the world and is readily recognized by anyone acquainted with jazz. This is equally true of other jazz soloists, famous or not.

CHAPTER 3

THE MUSIC OF THE SLAVES

Like all good stories, the story of jazz should begin at the beginning—which would be the days of slavery.

The idea of selling people into slavery is as old as civilization. Slaves existed in the ancient cultures of Egypt, Sumer, the Hebrew tribes, up through Greek and Roman societies to modern times. In Africa centuries ago, warring tribes enslaved their neighbors and Arab traders sold Negroes in the slave markets of North Africa and the Middle East. The intercontinental trade in slaves began in the 1400's when Portuguese explorers brought Negroes from Africa and sold them into slavery in Europe. (They said it was for the good of the Africans' souls!)

For the next four hundred years, the slave trade boomed. Explorers, travelers, sea captains and pirates found that rounding up hapless individuals in the jungles of South America or Africa and transporting them overseas was a very profitable business indeed. It has been estimated that some fifteen million African Negroes were sold in various parts of the world. A good portion of that number landed in America. The slaves were first introduced in the northern colonies, but as the tobacco and cotton economy in the southern colonies developed, large numbers of field hands were needed there. Eventually, it was from the slave population in Dixie that the minstrels, spirituals, country blues and our first sounds of jazz music came.

Music was all-important to the slaves. In Africa, village rituals had centered around dancing. Messages were sent with drumbeats, and jungle drums were an integral part of tribal ceremonies. The slaves brought with them to America a powerful sense of rhythm and melody. In the New World, music helped them endure a difficult life.

Since they owned no property and had no money to buy musical instruments, the slaves made do with what was at hand. Washtubs, bones that were clacked between fingers, washboards and homemade tambourines took the place of their native African instruments. The most important musical instrument of the American slave was the banjo. Quite a few historians believe the banjo came from Africa where it had been copied from a guitar-like instrument played by the Arabs.

There are several kinds of banjos. Some have four strings, some five, others more. The four-string banjo, today called the tenor banjo, was most popular with the slaves. The banjo was used often in the early jazz bands. Then during the 1930's and 1940's it went out of style and was rarely heard in jazz orchestras. There has been a revival of interest in the instrument in recent years, and once again it is highly popular.

The slaves played homemade instruments when they gathered around their cabins in the evenings after a hard day's work in the plantation fields. Their village chants and dances were far behind them and their owners discouraged African customs. So they began to absorb the music of their white masters. If they lived in Virginia,

Carolina, Delaware or other British-owned colonies they were exposed to European-Protestant musical traditions. They heard fiddling music that grew from Scottish bagpipe tunes, English hymns and lullabies and the folk songs—songs about lovers, God, the dramas of life, soldiers going off to war, folk heroes. One of these songs was a melody called "Frankie and Albert." It told the story of a gal who killed her man because he wouldn't treat her right. We still sing that tune, but today we know it as "Frankie and Johnny."

The slaves sang their own versions of the popular songs of the day along with their own style of spirituals and the blues.

Religion played an important role in the music of the slaves. The African was by nature a strongly religious person. Once in the New World he accepted Christianity readily enough, but fresh in his mind were African gods and religious dances and rituals. So he flavored his Christian worship with elements of the old African ceremonies. The fiery camp meetings that swept through the South in the 1800's had a great appeal to the slaves of Protestant faith because of their strong emotional pitch and stirring music. It was probably during this period that the Negro spiritual, which had such a strong influence on jazz, came into existence.

It was difficult for the Afro-American to participate in a religious service without rythm and dancing. Dancing was not permitted at Protestant church meetings but the slaves managed to get around the ban by inventing the "ring shout" which included handclapping and body movement to a rhythmic beat but was not exactly dancing. The ring shout took place when the hymn singing began. The slaves would stand up and start to move around a circle in a shuffling walk. Handclapping set up a beat that took the place of drums. Soon the entire congregation would be rhythmically moving in the circle as their voices were raised in song. Writers of that day who witnessed the phenomenon described its powerful emotional and hypnotic effect. Sometimes the slaves would sing for hours. Often worshippers would fall down in ecstatic seizures of religious fervor.

The religious music of the bygone days of slavery is important to the student of jazz because it traces the roots of rhythm and spontaneous melodic ideas.

"Lining out" was another manner of hymn singing favored by the slaves. The practice began in England in churches where many in the congregation could not read. The preacher who led the singing would read aloud a line from the hymnal and the congregation would then sing it. In this manner the group would go through an entire hymn with the leader keeping one line ahead of the singers. This practice was adopted by Negro Protestant congregations. Sometimes the leader or caller made up the lines as he went along. Many spirituals were composed in this spontaneous manner. Improvisation is also an important element of jazz music.

Another ancestor of jazz was the Negro slave's work song. He had learned that work went easier when done to music. Work songs were used by Negro field hands, stevedores, chain gangs and laborers in levee camps and on railroads. These work songs were performed in the call-and-response pattern of the hymn singing. The leader would sing a line and the workers would respond with an answering grunt or shout in unison. With each answering exclamation, the workers would swing their picks or heave on their ropes.

Here is an example of such a work song:

Leader: We gotta get this bad work done. Worker: Oh!
Leader: Never mind that hot ol' sun. Workers: Uh!
Leader: Boss man say, "Let's go!" Workers: Oh!
Leader: He mad if we move too slow. Workers: Uh!

A good work-song leader was highly regarded by workers and slave owners alike. Often making up the words of his song as he went along, he sang about his master or events in the daily lives of his friends—songs about work, love, trouble. For example, his song might be about the hero of a levee camp known for his strength and success with the ladies.

Slaves living in predominately Latin-Catholic territory, such as Louisiana, fell under the influence of a music and culture that was somewhat different from the English-Protestant tradition.

The Latin-Catholic cultures enjoyed colorful festivals, such as the flamboyant Mardi Gras celebration in New Orleans at which there was often music and dancing. These events became a part of the slave's experience too. The French-Spanish people in Louisiana loved parades and held them on many occasions. Parade music is a swinging 2/4 tempo closely related to jazz rhythm.

One of the favorite dances of the French-Spanish settlements in Louisiana during the nineteenth century was the quadrille. The music for the quadrille was played in 6/8 and 2/4 time. Both the music of marching bands and the dance rhythm of the quadrille had their effect on the early jazz of New Orleans which has essentially a 2/4 beat, or two strong beats to the measure. Some of the jazz melodies of New Orleans were taken directly from the quadrilles including the standard jazz classic "Tiger Rag."

In the Latin territories of the New World, the slave was freer to hold onto his native traditions and customs than was his brother in the Protestant colonies. For example, in New Orleans an area in the city called Congo Square was set aside so that the slaves could congregate on Sundays and dance in their native style to their hearts' content. At Congo Square the throbbing rhythms of Africa could be heard, while in another part of the city there might be a parade, somewhere else a quadrille, and a few blocks away a group of slaves singing hymns in rhythm 'n' blues style. It is small wonder that New Orleans eventually became the most important jazz city and the birthplace of so many great jazz performers: Louis Armstrong, King Oliver, Jelly Roll Morton, and many, many others down to our present day Al Hirt and Pete Fountain.

CHAPTER 4

THE MINSTRELS

On the stage a man dressed in frock-tailed coat of bright hue turns to a comedian on his left.

"Sam, how is your wife?"

"Compared to what?"

"Oh, now, Sam, don't talk that way. Your wife is a splendid woman. At least that's how she strikes me."

"Yes sir, and wif a skillet—that's how she strikes me!"

"Why, Sam, I think you are exaggerating. Just last week I was talking to her and she told me how much she misses you when you're away."

"Well, I reckon that is the truth—she do miss me when I'm away. But, my, what a dead aim she's got with that skillet when I'm home!"

There is laughter and applause from the audience. Then the master of ceremonies announces, "And now, ladies and gentlemen, that virtuoso of the banjo, Mr. Sam Bones, will play for you . . ."

On stage the white master of ceremonies called "the interlocutor" is flanked on either side by a row of comedians in blackface, the outer two called "end men." Behind them is a chorus of men and women. The scene and the type of entertainment was familiar on theater stages, in traveling tent shows and on showboats during the 1800's. This was a minstrel show, a uniquely American form of entertainment. Just as jazz is the only original American music, the minstrel show was America's first original contribution to the theater form. It was the most popular entertainment of that gaslit era from the early 1840's to about 1900. Out of it grew vaudeville, burlesque and the musical comedies of the twentieth century. The influence of the minstrel shows still echoes in today's television and motion picture programs.

The minstrel shows played a part in the early development of jazz. They carried the music of the slaves to the outside world, gave employment to many early jazz musicians and helped popularize ragtime, a predecessor of jazz. The minstrels were slapstick shows based on Negro stories, music and dances. Usually the Negro parts were played by white actors in blackface although there were some famous Negro entertainers too. On the whole, the minstrels were a burlesque of Negro life, presenting the Negro as a happy-go-lucky buffoon who nevertheless had a certain underlying earthy wisdom. The end men always managed to pull off the punch lines while the interlocutor remained a dignified straight man.

The minstrel shows developed as the theater tapped the great storehouse of entertainment in slave music and Negro lore. One of the first white men to stumble on the idea of blacking his face with burnt cork and appearing on the stage in a skit about American Negro life was Gottlieb Grouper. Grouper immigrated to Charleston, South Carolina, from Hanover, Germany in 1795. He was a capable musician who was fascinated by the music of the plantation slaves. In 1799, he appeared in blackface on the stage of the Federal Street Theatre in Boston and entertained with a collection of Negro songs and dances.

One of the most successful individual acts was performed by Thomas Dartmouth Rice who became a nationwide sensation when he introduced his "Jim Crow" song and dance in 1828. The first group to usher in the traditional minstrel-show style was the Virginia Minstrels in 1843. They were a quartet led by Daniel Decatur Emmett who composed a rousing minstrel "walk-around" number "Dixie," which became the battle song of the Confederacy.

Stephen Foster occupies such a hallowed place among American composers that we often overlook the fact that he wrote mainly for minstrel shows. Songs like "My Old Kentucky Home" and "Old Black Joe" were written for the Christy Minstrels, the most famous group of their day. Another well known group was Dockstader's Minstrels. Al Jolson began his career in show business with the Dockstader troupe.

The Christy Minstrels under the direction of E. P. Christy developed the standard minstrel-show format which changed little through the years. The program opened with a grand entrance in which the chorus and end men came on stage singing and dancing. Then the interlocutor gave the command, "Gentlemen—be seated!" A series of jokes was then exchanged between the interlocutor and the end men. From time to time, the horse play was halted for an instrumental number or a ballad or dance. This provided the first half of the evening's entertainment. The second part of the show was called the "olio." In it were featured various skits, musical virtuoso numbers and parodies on well known plays and operas. The finale usually brought the entire cast on stage in a musical "Plantation Festival" or a Cakewalk.

From the beginning, the minstrels used the traditional musical instruments of the slaves—the banjo, tambourine and bones. The end men were often called "Mr. Bones" and "Mr. Tambo" after these instruments. As the size of the troupes grew, the band grew and conventional orchestral instruments were added. By the 1850's most troupes had orchestras of twelve or more musicians, built around the nucleus of plantation Negroes' instruments. The happy twang of the banjo, the slap-rattle of the tambourine and the clacking of bones will forever be associated with minstrels.

One of the highlights of these shows was a dance called the Cakewalk. It was a high-stepping prancing walk with exaggerated bowing and hat doffing. Originally it was probably a sly spoof by the slaves of the grand Sunday manners of the white folks in the big plantation houses. The Cakewalk was performed to the gay, syncopated music of ragtime, a form of music highly popular around the turn of the century.

Although the minstrel and brass marching bands played ragtime, this style of music was especially the domain of the piano. Originating in the South and Midwest rather than specifically in New Orleans, the popularity of this catchy, rhythmic style quickly spread all over the world. In its heyday from 1890 to 1917, everyone was "ragging" the hit songs of the day; piano players in bars and honky-tonks all played ragtime.

The king of the ragtime pianists was a Negro Scott Joplin, who was born in Texarkana, Texas, in 1868, but made his home in Sedalia, Missouri. As a result, Sedalia became identified as the home of ragtime music. Scott Joplin studied music at the George Smith College for Negroes and thus had a formal background in harmony and composition. He composed many rags, the best known being the "Maple Leaf Rag" (1899) which he named after the Maple Leaf Club in Sedalia where he was playing when he wrote the tune.

Ragtime style is best described as heavily syncopated music—syncopation being a manner of accenting the normally weak beats in a measure. When playing ragtime, the pianist keeps up a steady 2/4 rhythm in the bass much like march tempo while his right hand emphasizes the unaccented or off beats. This sets up a multiple rhythm, or polyrhythm, between his two hands. The off-beat rhythm of one hand seems to bounce against the rhythm of the other with a resulting swingy, catchy gaiety. Unlike blues and jazz which can at times be melancholy, ragtime is always happy music. This type of playing probably grew most directly from the syncopated style of the plantation banjos of Negro slaves. The strong bass of ragtime piano players later developed into the stride-bass style of such great jazz pianists as James P. Johnson and Fats Waller. "Stride bass" is a piano style in which the left hand strikes bass notes on the strong first and third beats of a measure and the chord on the weaker second and fourth beats.

We associate ragtime music with the player pianos of grandfather's day, those fascinating instruments that only required the pumping of foot pedals to start a perforated paper roll turning and the keys rippling to produce the syncopated strains of "Twelfth Street Rag," "Down Home Rag" and other compositions of that era. Ragtime was the craze in the Gay Nineties, as rock 'n' roll is the craze of the 1960's. Today, when music is needed to set the mood for an old-time barroom scene in a movie or TV play, a tinkling, ragtime piano is often used.

In addition to ragtime, another feature of the minstrel shows was the trombone smear. The "smear" was a rousing type of show number in which the trombone player took advantage of the glissando, or sliding effect, he could produce with his instrument. It was a kind of cross between brass-band music and ragtime piano music. The brassy, audacious smear of the trombone, something like a Bronx cheer set to music, never failed to amuse audiences, and its syncopated rhythms set their feet to tapping.

Ragtime and brass-band numbers, like the trombone smear, were not yet jazz, but they were getting close. . . .

CHAPTER 5

THEY BEGIN PLAYING JAZZ

We decided to make a pilgrimage to the birthplace of jazz to hear the authentic story of how it began. Walking through the narrow, old streets of the French Quarter of New Orleans is like stepping into the past. Here among decaying buildings, balconies framed with iron grillwork, patios hidden from the streets, a visitor feels close to history. With very little imagination, he can project his mind into the past and hear the clippity-clop of horse-drawn carriages taking aristocratic ladies and gentlemen to the Opera House. He can see wagons loaded with cotton rumbling in from the plantations and the paddle-wheel steamboats tied up at the docks. He can hear gossip in French about a duel that was fought over a matter of honor.

The visitor can also hear the sound of New Orleans jazz; but this takes no imagination, for it floats out of many doorways along Bourbon Street. No other city has the jazz heritage of New Orleans, and this is where one comes to hear it played as it was in the beginning. So much does New Orleans treasure its jazz background that it even has a jazz museum, the only one of its kind in the world. Here one can find such hallowed objects as the first cornet Louis Armstrong owned. In the museum, a visitor can pick up a telephone, dial a request and hear historic jazz recordings of immortals like King Oliver, Bix Beiderbecke and Bessie Smith.

Also, in the old part of the city, a jazz enthusiast can visit Preservation Hall in the evenings and hear traditional New Orleans jazz played by musicians who remember how it all started.

We paid a visit to an old-time musician. His address led us down a narrow, cobblestone street, through a patio where ferns and banana trees were growing, up a rickety stairway to a small apartment that had a pleasant view of the rooftops of the old French city.

Our musician friend greeted us at the door. "I just put the coffee pot on," he smiled. "I make it Louisiana style, good and black with plenty of chicory. Hope you like it that way."

It takes some getting used to, that thick, bitter-black witches' brew they call coffee in New Orleans. But what else could one drink on an afternoon like that, with a fine mist drizzling on the ancient walled patio and rooftops and the talk about jazz going on in the cozy apartment.

We glanced around the room at a battered upright piano, stacks of music and books, a portable record player and a bookcase filled with records, a picture on the wall of Louis Armstrong bearing a scrawled signature, "Your friend, Satchmo." It was a nice apartment, pleasantly cluttered, and you felt that immortal jam sessions must have taken place here.

Our old musician friend moved to the window, sipping his coffee. "It's beginning to change, you know," he said sadly, "this old French section of town. They're tearing down some of the fine old buildings. I guess they didn't have much choice about some of them—they were falling down anyway. But it's a shame to see these old things change. People ought to keep ahold of the past in all the places they can. Once they're gone, nothing can ever put them back."

Then he smiled, "But you didn't come here to talk about that. You want to hear how we started playing this music down here." He took a chair, carefully placed his cup on a table beside him and leaned back, closing his eyes thoughtfully. This is the story he told us. . . .

If you really want to understand the beginning of jazz in New Orleans, you need to understand the way the people in this city live, the way they enjoy good food, good music and a happy way of life.

You see, New Orleans started off being a music town when it still had walls to keep out the Indians. The French, who owned Louisiana then, had soldiers garrisoned here to fight the Indians, and those soldiers had a spit-and-polish, bright-and-shiny, French military marching band. Those pioneer French settlers liked nothing more than to hear their military band come parading down the street. I guess the Indians liked to hear them, too.

You want to remember that the people who settled New Orleans were a little different from the settlers in other states. In New England, Virginia and the other English colonies, you had hard-working people like the Puritans. You had Scotch-Irish planters and frontiersmen, who probably didn't get around to taking a bath but once a year; good people, but kind of on the rough-and-ready side —you know, like Daniel Boone. The people who came to New Orleans included aristocrats from France and Spain. When Napoleon was in exile, some of those New Orleans aristocrats had a big plot going to bring him here. They even had a house ready for him.

The point is, when these people came to settle in the

New World, they brought some of their culture with them. On the sailing ships, they brought their crystal chandeliers, their family heirlooms, silver and fine furniture, and their harpsichords, violins and flutes and their books. They didn't come here planning to wear coonskin caps and live in log cabins. They built themselves a little European city in the wilderness of the New World, on the banks of the Mississippi. And it wasn't long before New Orleans was known as the most cultivated city in the New World. They had fine restaurants, just as they do now, and a highly developed society and culture. The first opera company in the United States was right here in New Orleans in the early 1800's. They had a symphony orchestra, too, at a time when pioneers in other states were playing jew's harps and spitting tobacco juice out of their log-cabin windows. Of course there were fine colleges and culture going on in other parts of the country too, but it just seemed that New Orleans had a special interest in all the good things of life, from food to music. New Orleans was pretty much a tolerant city, too; and for the most part, the feeling between the colored and white races was a friendly one.

The Civil War brought many changes to the city, and this all had a bearing on how jazz started. You see, when the field slaves were emancipated, many of them walked off the plantations and hit the roads, drifting toward cities where they could find jobs. They brought with them those old slave work songs, spirituals, field shouts and blues that were so much a part of Negro life. Well, they did find jobs in New Orleans. And when they walked down Rampart Street they saw all bright and shiny, in pawnshop windows, the musical instruments they'd seen white men play in the brass marching bands. The music that was in their souls gave them a terrible itching to own those instruments, and for the first time they had money to buy them.

Up until then, the slaves had to make their own

instruments because a slave had no money and could own nothing. They'd done the best they could with washtubs, gourds, bones and things like that. The traditional instruments of the slaves were the banjo and harmonica. Usually he'd make his banjo and his master might give him a harmonica. But now, all of a sudden, he could get his hands on real musical instruments—cornets, trombones, tubas, clarinets, violins, drums.

Now, that ex-slave didn't have any formal musical training. He'd take home the instrument he'd just bought and fondle it, messing around with the keys and mouthpiece. He probably got some terrible sounds out of it at first, but he had a native instinct about music and a musical ear to guide him, and pretty soon he was making music. Nobody taught him. He couldn't read a note. He didn't have any idea what key he was playing in. You see, he made that instrument an extension of his voice, and it sang for him. This idea of playing the way you sing is very important in understanding jazz. It's one of the things that makes jazz different from classical music, one reason some jazz sounds just can't be written down.

Once he got the feel of his instrument, the Negro played familiar music, the humming and singing of the field hands and the blues he might have heard once as he walked past a jailhouse window. He got the beat for his music from marching bands and church music, the handclapping, foot-stomping, gonna-walk-all-over-God's-heaven kind of spirituals. He wasn't hampered by the discipline of European musical training that was apt to make a man self-conscious. Improvising—making up his musical ideas as he went along—came naturally to the Negro. In Africa, his ancestors had composed their drum rhythms, dance steps and songs extemporaneously. In slave days, he had made up work songs in the field. In revival meetings he'd often been so inspired, and got religion so strong, that he'd composed spirituals on the spot, the words just seeming to spring from his lips. When he made music, he got it from the poetry in his soul. So why change now, just because he was singing with a cornet or trombone?

There's another important thing to know about at the time following the Civil War, and that was the lodges —secret societies you might say, or you could call them benevolent societies. More than a hundred of them sprang up, and they played a big part in Negro life—and incidentally, early jazz music. The reason for them was they gave the newly-freed black man a social life and a measure of security. One of their functions was to provide burial insurance. As long as the Negro had been a slave, he hadn't had to worry about funeral expenses. When he passed away, his master would see to his burial. But now he was on his own, and the expense of a funeral was sometimes more than an individual could afford. By joining a lodge and paying small monthly dues, the member was assured of a stylish funeral when the time came.

The funerals put on by the benevolent societies were really something. The brothers and sisters of those lodges were put away in style. First there would be a wake which might go on for several days and nights. The departed lodge member was laid out in high fashion. There are some lines from that fine old jazz number "St. James Infirmary" that describe how a lodge brother wanted to be laid away: in a box back coat, straight lace shoes and stetson hat.

Nobody tried to hold back his emotions at these wakes. There'd be weeping and wailing you could hear for blocks. Sisters would be passing out right and left. Refreshments were always served, potato salad, cold cuts, things like that—right along with plenty of smelling salts. The truth is, it was probably a lot healthier to carry on openly that way. Folks don't get nervous breakdowns from letting go of their feelings. It's holding them back that gets them in trouble.

Well, I guess you could say it was at the lodge funerals that the bands first started playing jazz. That's a peculiar way for it to begin, but that's how it was. You see, as far back as 1880 they had music at funerals, especially if the deceased belonged to a lodge. Those lodges hired a band to play a dirge behind the hearse as it went to the cemetery. There were no automobiles then. People walked in the funeral procession through the narrow streets. Following the wake, when the funeral procession would form, the lodge's band would take its place, everyone looking dignified and solemn. The black, horse-drawn hearse would take the lead. Somebody would carry the lodge banner, a splendid-looking velvet emblem with red and green lettering and a lot of silver trim. The band would play a slow, sad hymn like "Nearer My God to Thee."

New Orleans seems to have its own way of doing everything, and that includes burying. If you've gone by a New Orleans cemetery, you've noticed all the tombs above the ground. This city is built on such marshy ground that you can't dig a grave without having it fill up with water, so they must bury above the ground.

At the cemetery, there'd be the final services and a last outburst of emotion with some more fainting and usually at least one of the mourners throwing himself or herself across the coffin. Then everybody would form up outside the cemetery and start home, and the procession would wind away from the cemetery with the band in front. After they got a couple of blocks away, all of a sudden the drummer would unmuffle his snare and the band would start playing again. This time their music was different. Wasn't anything slow or sad about it. They played hymns and marches in quick, 2/4 time, tunes like "Didn't He Ramble," or "When the Saints Go Marching In." In those days they still called it ragtime, but it was more than ragtime, it was early jazz. The musicians had their own ideas about what they were playing—improvising, you see, which is the heart of jazz. I guess a bandmaster hearing them would have said they were embellishing the melody.

They didn't mean anything disrespectful or irreverent by playing jazz on the way home from the funeral. They believed in the saying "Rejoice at the death and cry at the birth." They figured a man is born into a life of misery and trouble; but when he passes on, he's gone to heaven where there's eternal happiness, so why not rejoice for him? Besides, that step-lively kind of ragtime-jazz was a sort of emotional release after the weeping and carrying on and tension of the funeral.

When those funeral bands marched home playing like that, they'd pick up big crowds of people who just followed to get in on the music, clapping their hands and dancing in the street. They called those people the "second line."

There was another element in some of these secret, fraternal lodges in New Orleans, and we might as well touch on it to get the whole picture. That element was voodoo, or hoodoo, or vodun, as it can be called. If you list the things that have a distinctive New Orleans flavor, you'd write down shrimp gumbo, pralines, Mardi Gras, Dixieland jazz and voodoo. Back in the days we're talking about, voodoo superstitions were a big thing in New Orleans, and there's probably some of it around today.

Voodoo was brought here by some of the early slaves from the West Indies, who brought it first from Africa. The best known voodoo queen of those earlier days was Marie Laveau. Some of the early jazz musicians, like Jelly Roll Morton, were strong believers in voodoo. Since the practice of voodoo was a form of African superstition and religion involving witch doctors, incantations, secret ceremonies and that sort of thing, it was considered heathen and was outlawed by the white authorities. That didn't keep it from being practiced in secret meetings. Sorcery and conjuring were all part of voodoo. A voodoo witch doctor could mix up a love potion or cast a hex on a person by sticking pins in a doll-sized figure of the victim. The witch doctors were supposed to be able to cure diseases or make good-luck charms.

A voodoo ceremony taking place in secret would consist of either the witch doctor or voodoo queen and a group of believers. There would be chanting and the rhythmic stamping of feet, clapping of hands and beating of drums until the rhythm had whipped the group into a frenzy, some of them falling down in twitching, frothing fits. This powerful element of African and West Indian rhythm was the link between voodoo and jazz.

Voodoo flourished because most of those freed slaves were uneducated, superstitious people. Such simple folk live close to the imaginary world of hobgoblins, fairies and witches. They are apt to have a spontaneous, creative imagination uninhibited by convention and unspoiled by too much civilization. From their unhampered imaginations came a freedom of expression and a strong, flowing river of emotion that breathed poetry into jazz and blues.

Funerals weren't the only places where the New Orleans brass bands were playing. The musicians in those early years of jazz—the late 1800's and early 1900's—found jobs all around the city. You know that was when America was enjoying a craze for brass bands. Every city had a weekly band concert in the park. But in New Orleans, the bands played music in their own style, which was jazz. In addition to funerals, they played for parades, carnivals, dances and at honky-tonks. They played for riverboat excursions on the Mississippi. The bands became well known around the city and jealous of their reputation. There was the Excelsior Brass Band, the Eagle Band, the Olympia Band and many, many others.

Quite often, when they wanted to advertise a dance they were going to play for, the bands rode through the streets in wagons, playing loudly to attract attention. They had some trouble with the trombone player because there wasn't room on the wagon for his slide to move without hitting another musician. They solved that by lowering the tail gate and the trombone player sat back there, his feet dangling, so he had plenty of room. To this day, they call the Dixieland style of trombone playing "tail gate" trombone. There's even a tune called "Let the Tail Gate Down." Any band on Bourbon Street knows that one.

When those bandwagons rolled down the streets, they'd attract crowds that followed along, clapping and singing. Sometimes they'd meet a rival wagon and there was sure to be a battle. They'd lock wheels and hold a "carving" contest, a war between the bands fought with music rather than knives. The crowds were happy when this happened. People would come running from all over, knowing they were going to hear some music. Well, those two bands would try to see who could play the loudest, the longest and the hottest. Finally the loser, winded and exhausted, would slink off defeated and humiliated. The winning band was sure to get the biggest dance crowd that night because people like a winner. Carving contests between bands and individual musicians became a jazz tradition. They happened all the time in New Orleans. Trumpet player Mutt Carey once said, "If you couldn't blow a man down with your horn, at least you could use it to hit him alongside the head."

The earliest jazz band in New Orleans was led by cornetist Buddy Bolden. Old-timers say he played the most powerful horn in history and never lost a carving contest.

Buddy played before they made phonograph recordings so there's no way of telling for sure just how good he was. Some say he may have recorded on those old-time Edison cylinders, but nobody has been able to find them if he did. So, I guess we have to take the word of musicians who heard him, like jazz trumpet player Bunk Johnson, who played in Buddy's band. Judging by the lasting impression Buddy made, he must have been a remarkable musician. He was the first of a new kind of American folk hero you might say—the young man with a horn, the hot jazzman, the king of popular music of his day.

Buddy Bolden was king during the late 1890's and early 1900's when music was in transition from ragtime to jazz. "Ragtime," although a first cousin to early jazz, was a more rigid, rhythmic style of heavy syncopation played with a fast, energetic march beat. Almost any tune could be "ragged." While the jazz of Bolden's day was primitive, it nevertheless had a more subtle feeling for the syncopated beat, and it gave the musician freedom to improvise. Buddy probably played a combination of ragtime and early jazz, though he was supposed to be at his best when playing the blues. I guess if you tried to put your finger on a time and place and say, "Here is where jazz began," you might come close with Buddy Bolden's band; but don't get the idea that jazz was ever the exclusive invention of one musician. It was a new way of playing popular music that grew out of earlier forms. Buddy Bolden was the pioneer who led the way, and today's jazz forms owe a lot to him.

Buddy was born back in 1868. Like a lot of young Negro boys growing up in New Orleans, he probably went down to Congo Square on Sundays and listened to those African drums and watched the people dance. They say he attended a church where a handclapping, shouting congregation rocked the building. Growing up in this city, he was bound to have followed the military-style, brass marching bands. No doubt, he got his ideas about music from those sources. When he was a boy he shined shoes. When he grew older, he learned the barbering and printing trades by watching others. When he saved up enough money to buy his first cornet at the age of fifteen, he learned to play that, too, by teaching himself. He couldn't read music. Like so many jazz musicians of his time, he would learn a melody by hearing it played. This was the way the traditional jazz tunes of New Orleans were handed down from one musician to another. Buddy Bolden carried his musical library around in his head.

In the 1880's, Buddy formed his first band. Some jazz historians say he had a double bass, valve trombone, clarinet, guitar and cornet in the band. Other experts say there was also a violin and drums. I don't know—both versions could be right. Only one member of Bolden's band, the valve trombone man Willy Cornish, could read music. When a new tune would come into town, printed on sheet music, Willy played it for the other members of the band to learn by ear.

Buddy's band was the most popular in the city. They played polkas, quadrilles, ragtime tunes in early jazz style and they played the blues. Buddy was so much in demand he sometimes had six or seven bands playing at different engagements the same night; and he'd go from one to another, sparking the dance with his powerful horn. Some dance-hall owners would not rent their halls unless Buddy was hired to play for the dance. During the day, Buddy operated a barber shop and published a small scandal sheet called *The Cricket*.

Buddy Bolden was a tall, colorful character who wore flashy clothes and enjoyed life. They say he was such a lady-killer that when he marched down the street with his band, there were at least three women beside him, one to carry his coat, one to carry his hat and one to carry his horn when he wasn't playing. And the ladies fought for the honor.

Buddy liked to say that when he blew his horn he was calling his children home. So powerfully did he blow that he could be heard all over the city and out on the river. On a still night from blocks away, Buddy could be heard "calling his children." They'd come from the levees, the honky-tonks, the houses crowded close together on narrow streets to the hall where he was playing. His special numbers were, "Make Me a Pallet On the Floor," "Bucket's Got a Hole in It," "Careless Love" and "219 Took My Baby Away."

And then something began going wrong with Buddy. Some who knew him said he drank too much, others blame it on overwork. One day in 1907 when he was marching in a New Orleans funeral parade with the Allen Brass Band, trying to sound like the Angel Gabriel himself, something in Buddy's mind snapped and he ran amuck.

Like other jazz kings who followed him, Buddy Bolden's life ended in frustration and tragedy. The day his mind snapped in that parade he lost touch with reality, and his music was gone forever. He was committed to the Louisiana State Hospital and spent the last twenty-four years of his life there, hopelessly insane. He died in 1931, forgotten by everyone except the jazz musicians he had inspired.

CHAPTER 6

JAZZ MUSIC SPREADS

Our old musician friend paused in his story. "Another cup of coffee?"

"Yes, thanks."

The fine rain spattered against the window. Outside it was growing dark and the lights of the French Quarter were beginning to glow in the mist. "How about the music that followed Buddy Bolden?" we asked.

He nodded. "That's the way to understand the truth about jazz music, starting with those early days in New Orleans from 1900 to 1917. Let's have a little background music here to get us in the proper mood." He went over to his record player, carefully selected a disk and put it on the machine. "Here's an album by Bunk Johnson who once played trumpet in Buddy Bolden's band. There's a story about Bunk. For a number of years in the 1930's Bunk quit music altogether. Then in 1937, some people interested in jazz research found him working as a day laborer in the cane fields, neglected and forgotten. He couldn't even afford to have his teeth fixed so he could blow his horn. Well, they bought him a set of store teeth and a new horn and during the last years of his life, Bunk gained some recognition. That's him playing now."

We sat back and listened to the traditional New Orleans style of Bunk Johnson. Then we began talking again, and our old musician friend resumed his story about the early days of jazz:

From 1900 to 1917, there were three important places where jazz music was being played. First, there was the section of New Orleans called Storyville, named for Alderman Story, sponsor of a city ordinance which in 1879 established this official "Garden of Sin." Storyville was one of the most wide-open spots on earth. A lot of the early bands and piano players found work in the cabarets and honkytonks there. Then there were the steamboats that went up and down the Mississippi, hitting all the river towns. Bands from New Orleans played on a lot of those boats. The third place was Chicago, which came into the picture about 1917. Jazz was played in other places, too, but these three were the most important in the development of this new music.

In those early days, people associated jazz with the sinning that went on in Storyville and that was partly the reason jazz had a bad name at first. And then, too, it was "Negro" music, and that didn't sit so well with race-conscious people. Even some of the middle-class Negroes didn't care for it. They associated it with the rougher, lower-class Negroes. At Buddy Bolden's dances, around midnight, the "nicer" people went home and then Buddy really started playing the low-down blues and there was likely to be fights and trouble. After the majority of the jazz musicians left New Orleans and started playing in

Chicago during the 1920's, they mostly played in speakeasies where they were hired by gangsters. So you can see how jazz got off on the wrong foot all the way around.

Now, the way I said, it was the poor, low-class Negroes that first started playing jazz in New Orleans. They put all their feelings about their troubles in their music. But there was another class of Negro in New Orleans who contributed a great deal to jazz and gave it the first musical polish. This was the Creole of Color whose musical and social background was a lot different from the uneducated Negro's. He had been formally trained in music and could read notes. When he first came in musical contact with the darker musicians who were playing by ear in their strange way, the Negro Creole was bewildered.

Strictly speaking, in New Orleans the descendants of the French and Spanish settlers are called "Creoles." If there is also a strain of African blood mixed in, the person is a "Creole of Color" or a "Negro Creole." Probably his great-grandfather had been a French or Spanish plantation owner and his great-grandmother had been the owner's African slave mistress. He might be only one-eighth Negro and look white. For a time in the 1800's, the Negro Creoles enjoyed a high social status in New Orleans. They were free men, well-off financially, some of them even rich; those who could afford it sent their children to the best European schools. They had a certain place in the white social and cultural life of New Orleans and were respected. They had their own boxes at the opera, and they had very fine, highly trained, military-style bands that marched in the white parades downtown.

In 1894 laws were passed creating legal segregation for anyone having even a small amount of African blood. That was the downfall for the Creoles of Color. They were hard hit, socially and economically. From then on they were discriminated against just like the darker Negroes. They were slowly pushed out of their jobs. Their bands were no longer allowed to play in white parades or in the homes of rich whites. There was no place for the Creole Negroes to go except to the rougher, uptown district, to the saloons and honkytonks of Storyville where the darker Negroes were playing their low-down blues and jazz.

At first, even though they were technically fine musicians, the Creoles of Color could not play jazz. What was a man supposed to do when he sat in a band and there was no written music and nobody bothered to tell him what key they were playing in? The leader just started them off and there they went, every man for himself—and yet somehow it all came together. Most likely, a lot of the Creole Negroes thought this kind of music was beneath them. But sooner or later, they got the hang of playing jazz, and with their trained musicianship they gave it a polish it had lacked. They learned the idea of jazz from the uptown Negroes, and in turn, the self-taught Negroes learned better musical techniques from the Creoles. A lot of the Creoles of Color became very famous jazz artists: clarinetists Alphonse Picou and Barney Bigard, trombonist Kid Ory, pianist Jelly Roll Morton and many, many others.

Two of the most famous bands to come out of Storyville were Freddie Keppard's Original Creoles and King Oliver's Creole Jazz Band. They say Freddie Keppard was very jealous of anyone copying his style. When he played his cornet he kept a handkerchief over his hand so other musicians couldn't watch his fingering. He even refused to let his band be recorded, for fear of being copied. You see, by the 1920's phonograph records were the best way for a musician to learn the trade. To this day, young jazz musicians learn by playing along with records, copying the way other musicians are playing until they get the feel and idea of jazz. It's too bad Freddie Keppard was so jealous, because not making records kept him from becoming immortal.

After Buddy Bolden left the scene, the title King of the Jazz Musicians passed to Joe "King" Oliver, who played the most advanced cornet of his day. Right here might be a good place to stop and say a word about the difference between the trumpet and cornet. They look alike and sound alike and people are apt to get them confused. The main difference is that the cornet is somewhat shorter and stubbier than the trumpet and has a bigger, warmer tone. The trumpet has a brighter, more penetrating tone that carries better. The early brass bands and jazz musicians favored the cornet. Buddy Bolden, King Oliver and Freddie Keppard played the cornet; Bix Beiderbecke did too. Louis Armstrong played cornet in the early years of his career, later switched to trumpet. From the early thirties on, the trumpet became more poular, though some famous jazzmen like Bobby Hackett play the cornet today.

Now back to King Oliver. He was born on a Louisiana plantation in 1885 and moved to New Orleans when he was a boy. When he was in his teens, he worked as a butler in the home of a white family. It was probably this background that gave him the formal, polite attitude he had all his life. People who knew Joe Oliver say he was always a gentleman and his appearance was noble and distinguished. He did not chase women or drink whiskey. Oliver's only vice was eating good food in too large quantities.

He began his musical career on the trombone and switched to cornet. He had some music lessons and could read notes. This ability to read, it turned out, got in the way of his first musical job. He tried out for a place in the Eagle Band, but he didn't get the job because he had to have notes to read and the band, which played by ear, looked down on anyone who had to read music. There's a famous story in jazz circles about trumpet player Wingy Manone applying for a job. When asked if he could read, he said, "Yeah—but not enough to hurt my playing!"

Since reading seemed to be hurting young Joe Oliver's playing, he set about learning to improvise, first on hymns. In time, he was good enough to work with the jazz bands in Storyville. At that time, the two top cornet men in the district were Freddie Keppard and Emmanuel Perez. There were heated arguments going around about who was best and the competition finally resulted in one of the most famous carving contests in jazz legend. The story goes that one night Joe Oliver decided to prove who was the best. In the middle of a number, he stalked into the street and pointed his horn at Pete Lala's cabaret where Freddie Keppard was playing and blew with such inspiration and power that he "blew down" Freddie Keppard. Then he crossed the street and took on Emmanuel Perez. Again Oliver proved he was top man, and with that clearly established, he walked proudly down the street, blowing his horn to the sky with an excited crowd following him until he finally led them back to his cabaret still blowing his great horn. From then on he was always known as King Oliver.

During those Storyville days, King Oliver inspired and taught a youngster who one day was to outshine the King and be the single greatest influence on jazz music for decades to come. That youngster was Louis Armstrong. King Oliver owes much of his jazz immortality to two things—one, being the teacher of Louis Armstrong; and two, his Creole Jazz Band being the first Negro jazz group to make phonograph recordings.

Storyville, where King Oliver and so many other early jazz musicians played in the early 1900's, was like no other place on earth. Here in the gambling joints, saloons, honky-tonks and cabarets, a dozen or more bands worked every night. Until they opened this district, most musicians held other jobs during the day. But in Storyville jazz musicians found full-time work for the first time.

Storyville developed the jazz pianist. The earliest jazz bands were brass marching bands and they couldn't use a piano. But the honky-tonks in Storyville began hiring piano players. The greatest of those early piano men was Jelly Roll Morton. Jelly Roll used to earn fifteen to eighteen dollars a night at Lulu White's place in Storyville before he went on to fame. The Library of Congress had him sit down at the piano to play and reminisce about the early jazz days, and they recorded it all. Jelly Roll composed a number of classic jazz tunes, "King Porter Stomp," "Milenburg Joys," "Wolverine Blues," "London Blues" and others.

In 1917, the government decided that Storyville was getting out of hand. A lot of sailors were getting their heads bashed in behind cabarets in dark alleys, so they closed the district forever. That was a sad day for all the gamblers, sharpies, dance-hall girls and, especially, for the musicians who had been working there. New Orleans suddenly became a good place for a musician to starve, and the jazz boys hit the road—and the river. Some of them found jobs on excursion boats going up and down the Mississippi; others went into the Southwest, to Texas, and some up to Memphis.

One of the best places for musical opportunities was the South Side of Chicago where there were flourishing nightclubs. That's where many of the New Orleans musicians landed, among them King Oliver. The King left New Orleans in 1918 and started working in Chicago. Late in 1919, he took over a band which he re-named the Creole Jazz Band. It became the top Negro jazz group of that time. In 1922, King Oliver sent for Louis Armstrong who joined the band to play second cornet. The following year the band had its famous recording session for Victor—famous because no Negro jazz band had done anything like it before. The records they made are considered masterpieces of the New Orleans-style jazz of that time. Some of the tunes they cut were "Mabel's Dream," "Dippermouth Blues," "Weather Bird Rag," "Chimes Blues," "High Society," "Sobbin' Blues," "Where Did You Stay Last Night" and "Snake Rag." The band's lineup for the recording date, beside Oliver and Armstrong, included Honoré Dutrey (trombone), Johnny Dobbs and Jimmie Noone (clarinet), Baby Dodds (drums), Bill Johnson (bass), John St. Cyr (banjo) and Lil Hardin (piano).

Joe Oliver went on being king until 1928 when things began going downhill for him. He started having dental trouble, which is death to a cornet man, and he had to hire other cornet players to take his solos. He did some band tours which flopped badly. Finally, in the early 1930's, he settled in Savannah, Georgia and faded out of the music scene.

That's how New Orleans and Chicago figured in the jazz picture during those particular years, but you don't want to forget the riverboats. A lot of fine, hot jazz was played on the decks of those old stern-wheel and side-wheel paddle boats that went from New Orleans to Memphis and points north. The owners of the boats noticed the passengers liked to hear the deck hands play their harmonicas and banjos at night after the work was done. So they started hiring regular bands to go along on the river trips. The best known of the riverboat bandleaders was Fate Marable. Fate was a piano player who sometimes played a steam calliope on the boats. He hired some top jazz stars to play in his bands, men like Louis Armstrong, Red Allen, Zutty Singleton, Johnny and Baby Dodds, Emmanuel Perez and Johnny St. Cyr.

The important thing to us about the riverboats was they spread the New Orleans style northward. People in other towns along the river got to hear this new kind of music and they liked it. There was a high-school boy named Bix Beiderbecke up in Davenport, Iowa, who heard jazz for the first time on those riverboats and he became the idol of jazz musicians in the 1920's.

Our old musician friend stood up. "Well, I guess that's about all I can tell you tonight about the early days. There's a lot more to it, of course, a lot more names and great musicians. It would take too long to cover every little detail, but you've got the general idea."

We said good night and walked downstairs into the dripping night. For a moment, we stood on the dark sidewalk, wondering what it must have sounded like the night King Oliver stood in that New Orleans street and blew Freddie Keppard down.

CHAPTER 7

THE ORIGINAL DIXIELAND JASS BAND

Up to this point in our study of jazz music, we have talked mainly about the contributions made by the American Negro, and for good reason. Generally speaking, when something new and fresh is heard in jazz, it comes from the Negroes' rich musical imagination. Too, jazz music from its earliest days has reflected the social struggles and attitudes of the Negro.

Through his work songs, the slave gave expression to his despair at the never ending, backbreaking labor. His spirituals were the crying out of an oppressed people for the promised land. Early jazz was an emotional safety valve for his frustrations at trying to cope with the white man's world. The bop and cool jazz movements in the 1940's and 1950's reflected the Negroes' rejection of the so-called Uncle Tom manner of trying to please the white man by conforming to the stereotyped image the white man had of the Negro. These later jazz trends reflected a growing communal spirit among Negroes. Especially among the young intellectuals, there was a new pride in their race, a desire not to make themselves into middle-class white Americans who happened to have black skin, but to be distinctly Negroes, proud of their African heritage.

In view of this, one could say that much of the Negroes' jazz has been protest music—protest against oppression and bondage, against poverty and despair, against his position in society. Perhaps this is what has given Negro jazz such vitality: people who are engaged in a struggle, who feel themselves oppressed, are often driven to greater inspirational heights than the comfortably complacent.

However, despite the obvious importance of the Negro in jazz, it would be seriously one-sided to overlook the tremendous contributions of white musicians to jazz. Some musicologists go so far as to insist that the African element in jazz has been overstated, that jazz is more European than African. They take the view that the musical forms used in jazz are taken from the European tradition. For example, jazz music is based on melodies that have twelve, sixteen or thirty-two bars. This division has grown out of the traditional European-American folk songs, English-Scottish-Irish ballads, Protestant hymns and military marches. The scale most used in jazz is the diatonic scale of European tradition rather than the African pentatonic scale. And the harmonies are of classic European design. Perhaps it is sensible to take the middle ground. Without the African influence and the Negro "soul" feeling, European-American music might not have producer jazz; but without European musical forms, African music would have remained African music, as widely separated from American jazz as the two continents themselves.

It is interesting to recall that while a great deal of the jazz being played in New Orleans in the early 1900's came from Negro musicians, it was a group of white jazz musicians, who first carried the message of jazz to the outside world and became the first world-renowned jazz band.

They called themselves the Original Dixieland Jass Band and they made the first jazz recordings in history, in 1917, five years before King Oliver recorded in Chicago. Furthermore, while the music they played grew out of Negro jazz being heard in New Orleans, there was a somewhat different style and sound. Their way of playing is what we call today the Dixieland style.

If we were to hear Buddy Bolden's band today, it would sound raw and primitive, with all the musicians improvising at the same time, giving out shouts, growls and hollers on their horns, the way they would with their voices if they were singing. The New Orleans bands which followed Bolden—Freddie Keppard, King Oliver and others—were smoother, but they kept the strong Negro blues influence along with an echo of the marching bands, in a style that is still called "traditional New Orleans jazz." Some music experts insist that if you want to hear this real traditional jazz today you'll have to hear it played by old-timers in New Orleans. It has a primitive, original sound compared to highly polished modern jazz and swing.

Today when a musician uses the term Dixieland, he has a definite style and form in mind. A Dixieland band has a trumpet (or cornet), trombone and clarinet in the front line, backed up by a rhythm section of drums and piano; there can be a bass (string bass or tuba), and there may be a banjo or guitar. This instrumentation goes back to the marching bands. The trumpet-trombone-clarinet combination symbolizes the various sections of a marching band distilled to one man representing each section. Dixieland, again in the strict definition of the word, is played in a two-beat tempo: two strong, bass beats to the measure like the sound of march music. The best Dixieland drummers can produce a crisp press roll on their snares like parade drummers.

In a Dixieland rendition, first the whole ensemble

plays the tune with the lead trumpet punching out the refrain in a strong, rhythmic, syncopated style adhering closely to the melody line. The clarinet man is improvising above the trumpet—notes that put in a nice pattern of musical embroidery.

Webster's defines counterpoint as: "One or more independent melodies added as accompaniment to a primary melody." This is a good definition of what is going on in a Dixieland band. The trumpet is playing one melody, the original strain. The clarinet is improvising a different sort of melody at the same time; this second musical line is related to, but independent of, the melody the trumpet is playing. At the same time, the trombone is improvising yet a third melody line in what might be called a semi-bass style, with a tail-gate smear or growl now and then.

While all this counterpoint is going on between the trumpet, clarinet and trombone, the rhythm instruments (drums and piano) are laying down a solid pattern of chords and beats.

After the entire ensemble plays a chorus of the melody in the contrapuntal fashion described above, the musicians take turns playing jazz solos. Here is where they really go to town and show how inventive they can be. The more inspired the musician is by the rhythm and the mood of what is going on, the more exciting his jazz solo. The notes he plays are not those someone else wrote down —they are coming out of his own head and heart at the moment. After each soloist has spoken his piece, the whole group gets together for a final rousing ensemble chorus or two, and the drive and excitement build to a climax. This is known as hot Dixieland jazz. The white musicians who came from New Orleans played in this style.

George Vitelle Laine, a white drummer known as "Jack" or "Papa," assembled his first band in New Orleans in 1888, about the time Buddy Bolden appeared on the jazz scene. Papa Laine claimed his band was the first to play a ragtime style. (The early New Orleans bands called their music ragtime until the word jazz began to be used in a musical sense around 1915).

Through the early years of jazz in New Orleans, Laine booked a number of bands that played in parades, on advertising bandwagons and for parties and dances, in the same fashion as the colored bands described earlier. Almost every white jazz musician in the city played in one or more of Laine's bands. Before World War I, Laine directed the Reliance Brass Band made up entirely of white musicians from New Orleans. In 1951, the New Orleans jazz club proclaimed Laine, who was by then seventy-seven, the "first white jazz musician."

When the first group of Papa Laine's musicians ventured north to Chicago with their new kind of music, jazz, or jass, was a slang word with a sordid meaning that had nothing to do with music. The term probably got its musical significance from these men. The story goes that Chicago musicians looked on the New Orleans intruders with a jaundiced eye fearing competition, and in an uncomplimentary manner said the wild, raucous music they played was a bunch of jass, or more accurately that they "jazzed" music. Whether the legend is true or not, the group was booked into Lamb's Cafe in Chicago under the name of Brown's Dixieland Jass Band, and they were a rousing success. That was some three years before King Oliver arrived in Chicago.

Some of the personnel of Brown's Dixieland Jass Band formed the Original Dixieland Jass Band under the direction of cornet player Nick LaRocca. In 1917 they were booked into Reisenweber's Cafe just off Columbus Circle in New York City. This event turned out to be a milestone in jazz history. The band made a tremendous impact; their music was revolutionary. Overnight jazz swept the country. Every nightclub and cafe had to have a jazz band to please the newly jazz-hungry public. It was the start of a whole new era called the Jazz Age: a social phenomenon, a decade when jazz music was the theme song of a nation gone wild with prosperity, the days of flappers, speakeasies, bathtub gin and raccoon coats.

As previously stated, The Original Dixieland Jass Band was the first jazz group to make phonograph records. They made their debut on the Victor label in February 1917 recording two tunes, the "Livery Stable Blues" and "Dixie Jass Band One-Step." Shortly after this they recorded their most popular numbers "Tiger Rag," "Ostrich Walk," "At the Jazz Band Ball," "Sensation Rag" and "Skeleton Jangle." The best-known jazz tunes originated and recorded by this band were "Clarinet Marmalade," "Fidgety Feet" and "Barnyard Blues." The tunes recorded by the group became classics and are to be found in the repertoire of almost every Dixieland group since that time. The musicians in the band included beside LaRocca, Henry Ragas on piano, Eddie "Daddy" Edwards on trombone, Larry Shields on clarinet and Tony Sbarbaro on drums.

These recordings had a fantastic effect on popular music. Musicians in the most isolated parts of the country could hear New Orleans Dixieland jazz and learn the new style. In the Midwest, youngsters like Bix Beiderbecke undoubtedly listened to these records by the hour and were more influenced by them than by any other source. From the style of the Original Dixieland Jass Band, Chicago-style jazz was developed by young, white musicians in the 1920's.

Dixieland, an off-shoot of traditional New Orleans jazz, led to Chicago style in the 1920's and that led to Swing in the 1930's. The work of talented white musicians was strongly felt in these three forms of jazz.

CHAPTER 8

SATCHMO

The year is 1923. A group of young white musicians has gone to the Lincoln Gardens, a nightclub on the South Side of Chicago, to hear King Oliver's band. In the crowd is Hoagy Carmichael, he of the long, somber countenance who is to be immortalized by his composition "Stardust." With him are a round-faced young man who plays cornet Bix Beiderbecke, who will be a legend before many years have passed, and another musician friend Bob Gillette.

What happened that night when the band started playing is best described in Hoagy Carmichael's own words:

> "The King featured two trumpets [actually two cornets], piano, a bass fiddle, and a clarinet. . . . Bix gave the sign to a big black fellow, playing second trumpet for Oliver, and he slashed into "Bugle Call Rag."
>
> "I dropped my cigarette and gulped my drink. Bix was on his feet, his eyes popping. For taking the first chorus was that second trumpet, Louis Arm-

strong. Louis was taking it fast. Bob Gillette slid off his chair and under the table. He was excitable that way.

" 'Why,' I moaned, 'why isn't everybody in the world here to hear that?' I meant it. Something as unutterably stirring as that deserved to be heard by the world."

Such was the emotional impact of Louis Armstrong's dramatic horn on his contemporaries. The unrivaled significance of this genius of American jazz on the musical world is well described in a feature story about Louis Armstrong, which appeared in *Life* in 1966:

> "Louis Armstrong behind his trademarks—his mugging, that grand piano smile, that iron filings voice—is an authentic American genius. It is a simple fact of jazz music, the only art form America ever wholly originated, that virtually all that is played today comes in some way from Louis Armstrong. . . . More than any other individual, it was Armstrong who took the raw, spontaneous folk music of the honky-tonks and street parades and, quite unconsciously, built it into a music beyond anything musicians had previously imagined."

In the latter part of his career, Louis Armstrong became better known as a singer and entertainer than as a jazz soloist, but by then his influence on all popular music was a matter of history. The early parade bands of New Orleans, the Original Dixieland Jass Band and the Chicago bands of King Oliver's era played their jazz mostly in the style of collective improvisation. It was Armstrong who raised the jazz solo to never dreamed of heights. The originality and dramatic beauty of his improvisations and the rich quality of his tone defy description.

To hear the trumpet of Louis Armstrong on its wildest flights one must turn back to his recordings made in the late 1920's, although any time Satchmo raises his horn to his lips one is in for a rich musical experience.

Louis Armstrong was born on the Fourth of July, 1900, in New Orleans, a suitable birthdate for a man who has become an American institution in this century. When he was hardly past the toddling stage, Louis was already drawn to the sound of music. He used to slip down to a dance hall nearby on Perdido Street and peep at the dancers through cracks in the wall while he listened with childish wonderment to the rough New Orleans-style jazz. He was one of the urchins who formed the second line behind the street bands. His favorite band was the Onward Brass Band and his hero was Joe Oliver.The proudest moment of his young life was when Joe Oliver let him walk along beside him in a parade and carry his horn when he wasn't playing.

Music was all around the young Louis Armstrong, an integral part of his life and the life of the city of his birth. Even the tradespeople had their music: the waffle man came around blowing jazz on a bugle and the pie man, the junk man and the banana man made their rounds singing and playing some kind of instrument; no matter how crude or battered it was, they made it swing. Louis, himself, worked as a youngster on a coal wagon and sang right along with the best of them. "Buy your stone coal—just a nickel a bucket!" He carried his buckets of coal to the back doors of the honky-tonks and dance halls of Storyville and heard the jazz being played there. At the age of twelve when he wasn't selling coal, Louis sang tenor in a quartet of youngsters who earned nickels and dimes singing on street corners.

One New Year's Eve Louis was out singing with the quartet, and became so carried away with the festive mood of the evening that he smuggled his stepfather's .38 pistol out of his house and fired it into the air in a burst of sheer exuberance, bang-bang-bang! He only intended to welcome in the New Year, but the law didn't think a .38 revolver was a suitable noisemaker for a twelve-year-old. A heavy hand fell on Louis' arm; and he was taken off, sobbing and pleading, to a juvenile shelter. The juvenile court concluded that young Louis was running around in bad company and sent him to the waifs' home, thereby performing a great service to the future of American music, for it was here that Louis learned to play the cornet.

The bandmaster at the home, Peter Davis, had an eye on Louis and invited him to join the band. "I don't know how to play nothing—only sing," Louis admitted.

"Sing and shoot off .38 revolvers," the bandmaster agreed. "Well, you can start out on tambourine."

From tambourine Louis graduated to drum, and from that to the alto horn. His next musical step upward was the bugle, and he earned the undying hostility of the other children by lustily blowing reveille every morning. When the band's cornet player was released from the home, Louis fell heir to the instrument; and the bandmaster gave him lessons. The first melody he conquered was "Home Sweet Home." Soon Armstrong was the leader of the twenty-man band. It was good enough to play for many parades in town sponsored by the social clubs.

Louis spent a year and a half at the home before he was released in custody of his mother and stepfather. He had only reached the fifth grade in school, but he did not return, thereby becoming one of the country's most successful dropouts. His family needed money, and he was something of a child prodigy on the horn, already able to play professionally though still in short pants. When a band in town was short a cornet player somebody would say, "Run and get that little Armstrong kid."

Each time he played a job, Louis had to rent a horn —he couldn't afford to buy one. Finally, in Uncle Jake's pawnshop, he found a beat-up, nickel-plated cornet for ten dollars. Louis borrowed the money from a friendly white man, and he owned his first horn. His next horn came from his musical godfather King Oliver. After he was through playing one evening, the great King dropped into the club where young Louis was working. Oliver remembered the youngster who used to run beside him in the parades. He told Louis the beat-up horn he was playing was a disgrace and offered to give him one of his old horns. Louis was tearful with gratitude.

More and more, Joe Oliver took Louis under his wing. It is paradoxical that many musicians who work in places of vice and sin are themselves clean-living family men. Joe Oliver was such a man. He didn't drink or hang around saloons. He often invited Louis to his house where he stuffed the youngster with his favorite dish, red beans and rice. "Eat plenty of that, boy. Give you something to blow your horn with." Then when Louis was stuffed with good food, he'd get a music lesson from the King himself.

Louis has never ceased giving credit to King Oliver for helping him in his early career. On a Decca record jacket he calls Oliver "my friend, my teacher, and my inspiration."

In his teens, Louis took every playing job he could find. He gave everything he had to music, pouring his last ounce of strength into his horn, knocking himself out to please those who heard him. In his teens he was already getting a reputation for his high, clear notes. One night playing his heart out in a Memphis honky-tonk, reaching for one high note after another, he blew so hard he split his lip wide open and blood streamed down his shirt.

Louis always refers to his lips affectionately as

"chops," and the care he lavishes on his chops includes vast quantities of a salve made especially for him by a firm in Germany. Satchmo says he buys the ointment by the case and the remarkable notes he can still play attest to its usefulness.

By the time he was eighteen, Louis was playing nightly in honky-tonks frequented by tough characters who did not consider themselves fully dressed without a concealed gun or razor. Frequently bullets and chairs whizzed past Louis' head when a free-for-all erupted, and he learned, as do many musicians, that a bandstand is not the safest place in the world.

Traditionally, when a fight starts, the band is supposed to keep on playing. The reasoning is based on the questionable theory that the crowd will stop fighting and go back to dancing. What actually happens is the music usually inspires greater mayhem. A story is told about an evening when a particularly violent fight started, and the band broke into a fast version of "Tiger Rag." The trombone player, a timid soul, hid behind the piano. All that could be seen of him was his trombone slide darting out from behind the piano with a white handkerchief, a flag of truce, tied on the end.

Louis Armstrong experienced many such nights in the tough district where he was playing, but he managed to duck the flying missiles and keep on playing. He was making enough money by then to afford a John B. Stetson hat and a wife, a hot-tempered dance-hall girl named Daisy. During his short but hectic marriage to Daisy, Louis found himself ducking flying objects at home as well as on the bandstand. One day when Daisy caught Louis walking down the street with another girl, she took off after him brandishing a razor. Louis managed to escape by jumping a ditch, but in so doing he lost his Stetson. Daisy took out her jealous rage on the hat, slicing it into ribbons.

Louis apparently thought more of the hat than he did of Daisy, for that was the end of the marriage.

When Storyville was shut down in 1917, King Oliver left for Chicago. Louis took his place in Kid Ory's band. The following year, Louis played with Fate Marable's band on the riverboat "Sidney." In the band with Armstrong were Warren "Baby" Dodds on drums, George "Pops" Foster on bass, David Jones on mellophone, Johnny St. Cyr on banjo and guitar and Boyd Atkins on violin. They played on excursions out of New Orleans and St. Louis. In the spring they went to Davenport, Iowa. There musicians introduced Louis to a local boy named Bix Beiderbecke. At their first meeting Louis just thought he was a nice, white boy and it wasn't until later that Louis heard Bix play. By then Bix was having almost as much influence on jazz as Louis. While he was playing on riverboats, Louis met another young white musician: Jack Teagarden who became the trombone virtuoso of the blues and who later made many recordings with Armstrong.

Louis continued playing on riverboats until 1922 when once again he felt the hand of his idol Joe Oliver, helping him up the musical ladder. The King sent a telegram asking Louis to join his band in Chicago. That was a momentous day in the career of Louis Armstrong. It was in King Oliver's band at the Lincoln Gardens that Armstrong began to astound the jazz world with solos that had a lyricism and imagination never heard before.

But Louis was still in the shadow of his teacher. Together Oliver and Armstrong composed several famous numbers including the "Dippermouth Blues." At that time, Louis was called "Dippermouth," which was accurately descriptive, if not overly complimentary. Louis has had a number of nicknames, all referring to the generous proportions of his chops. It was the nickname "Satchelmouth," shortened to "Satchmo," that stuck and by which he is known the world over.

Louis stayed with Oliver in Chicago for two years. Then in 1924 Fletcher Henderson sent for him to play in his big New York band. It was in Henderson's band that Louis had the opportunity to record with such immortal blues singers as Bessie Smith and Ma Rainey.

After a year in New York, Louis returned to Chicago and played for a while in a fifteen-piece pit orchestra at the Vendome Theater. When he first got the job, Louis realized with some misgivings that he was going to have to read classical music, overtures from *Cavalleria Rusticana* and the like were performed by the orchestra to accompany the silent movies. "I don't know if I can cut that stuff," Louis confided to Lil Hardin who was to become the second Mrs. Armstrong. Lil, who had played piano with Oliver's band but also had a fine background of classical training, said, "Sure you can. I'll help you." And she did, working with him for many long hours. This brush with classical music made a lasting impression on Armstrong, and his jazz solos often contain bits and phrases of the music he played during that period.

It was during his time with this orchestra that Louis switched from the stubby cornet to the longer trumpet. Erskine Tate, leader of the orchestra, looked at him one day and said, "You sure look funny playing that little ol' sawed-off horn." Louis, always anxious to look good before an audience, promptly went out and bought a trumpet, which he played from that time on.

When Louis left Tate he opened with his own band in the Sunset Club, directly across the street from the club where King Oliver was playing. The owner of the Sunset, Joe Glaser [Louis' manager to this day] put on the marquee, "Louis Armstrong, World's Greatest Trumpeter." By then few would argue with the sign. Louis had even surpassed his idol. Night after night, Louis out-blew his friend and teacher and drew the crowds from Oliver's place to his; but the two great musicians remained friends. Louis' devotion to Joe Oliver is one of the most touching stories to come out of the jazz epoch.

After 1930 Louis Armstrong continued to rise in the entertainment world, but King Oliver went downhill. In 1937, when Armstrong's band was playing in Savannah, Georgia, Louis noticed a familiar figure operating a small vegetable stand. "Papa Joe . . . Papa Joe Oliver!" Louis cried, running up to his old friend. They shook hands warmly, both too choked with emotion to speak for a moment.

The King was down and out and broke; he'd had a succession of bad breaks as a bandleader, and even worse a case of pyorrhea [a severe disease of the gums] which ended his days as a cornet player. Now he had nothing left but his dignity and memories of past glories. Louis took up a collection for Joe among his band members, all of whom had at one time played for King Oliver. That night Oliver came to hear Louis' band. He had gotten his Stetson hat, box-back coat and high-button shoes out of the pawnshop and looked like the old King Oliver again.

Armstrong made so many memorable recordings that it would be hard to pick his best. However, those he made with his groups The Hot Five and The Hot Seven in the late 1920's on the Okeh label show his solo work at its best. Some jazz authorities believe these recordings were the first to put the spotlight on the jazz artist as a soloist, since earlier recordings presented jazz as more of a group effort.

The personnel of Armstrong's Hot Five were Johnny St. Cyr on banjo, Kid Ory on trombone, Johnny Dodds on clarinet and Lil Hardin—by then Mrs. Armstrong—on piano. Unfortunately, these early recording sessions took place before the development of hi-fidelity equipment so the true sound quality is lacking. This holds true for all recordings made during the early days of jazz and it is a pity, for today we can never be sure what musicians like King Oliver really sounded like. Fortunately, Louis Armstrong has made later recordings of tunes played by the Hot Five, and they can be heard in truer fidelity on such albums as "Satchmo . . . a Musical Autobiography of Louis Armstrong" (Decca Records, DXM-155).

Some interesting anecdotes developed out of Armstrong's Hot Five recording session. When Louis got up to the microphone to sing the lyrics on "Heebie Jeebies," he dropped the music which contained the words, so he made up his own words, many of them just sounds; and many believe this is how scat singing was born. In "scat" the jazz vocalist creates his own version of the melody using words or abstract phrases, frequently humorous, instead of singing the written lyrics. In other words, he improvises vocal hot licks much as he would on an instrument.

Later on in the recording session when the band played "Gully Low Blues," Johnny Dodds was supposed to run up to the microphone and shout, "Oh, blow it, Pappa Dip!" during an Armstrong break. Dodds was carefully rehearsed on the line. His big moment came and he got to the microphone on time, but his mouth flopped open and closed with no sound coming out. The band stopped and everyone stared at him. Dodds looked embarrassed. "I can't talk into that thing," he admitted. He could speak eloquently with his clarinet, but he'd been seized by stage fright when it came to talking into the mike. He retired in humiliation, and the line was given to Kid Ory.

Louis' singing, like his playing, is in a class by itself. His voice has all the tonal finesse of a tractor transmission with a faulty bearing, and yet he is one of the most popular vocalist of all time. The notes he sings are as true as the notes he plays; and in some amazing fashion he manages to sing the same jazz licks he blows on his horn. An Armstrong vocal has much the same phrasing and quality as an Armstrong trumpet solo.

The hard, traveling life of a jazzman—irregular hours, dissipation, automobile accidents, alcohol and drugs—wrecked the health and took the lives of many jazz immortals at early ages. Fortunately, Louis has escaped the early tragic downfall that haunted the careers of other jazz heroes—cornetist Buddy Bolden, incurably insane at an early age; bandleader King Oliver, his career wrecked by gum disease; cornetist Bix Beiderbecke, dead of pneumonia at twenty-eight; clarinetist Frank Teschemacher, killed in an auto crash when he was twenty-seven; saxophonist Charlie Parker, addicted to narcotics and dead before he reached the age of thirty-five; and the great blues singer Bessie Smith, killed in an auto crash in Mississippi while on tour. The list could go on and on.

Louis Armstrong, however, loves life and music and has the good sense to take care of himself so he can enjoy both as long as possible. He does this with a wide assortment of vitamins and home remedies. He swears by a foul-tasting herbal laxative called Swiss Kriss, because he says "it's important to clear out the system." He takes this heroic dose with a chaser of bourbon almost nightly. When he comes off stage, dripping wet after a performance, he gives his back and chest a liberal swipe with a patent medicine called Heet to dry and warm his skin. For eye comfort, he recommends gauze pads dipped in witch hazel and placed on the eyelids for several minutes. Heart pains he attributes to gas, and he grabs a bottle of stomach medicine upon any sign of stomach distress. He never leaves his trumpet mouthpiece lying around dressing rooms "where germs can crawl all over it." It's in his pocket when he is not playing. One of his friends remarked that the care Satchmo takes of himself would long ago have killed a lesser man! By way of reply, Armstrong points out that he's still going strong while most of the early New Orleans musicians of his generation are long dead and gone. He confesses, though, that considering his age, he's taken to reading the Bible regularly!

Still, Satchmo's career continues to thrive with motion picture roles, hit records, world tours and television shows (he is paid twenty to twenty-five thousand dollars for guest appearances on television). He still plays all the old New Orleans traditional-jazz tunes, but he also takes on currently popular songs and gives them his special treatment. There is always the sly Armstrong spoofing of the trite lyrics, a sparking of the banal melody line, the cheerful clowning, and it comes out an entertainment gem. A testimony to Armstrong's durability is his recording of "Hello Dolly!" Made in his sixties at a time when most of the New Orleans jazz men of his time were gone and forgotten, Armstrong came up with one of the greatest hit records of all time.

His own words [from a biography in *Harpers*] best describe the feeling that goes into an Armstrong jazz trumpet solo:

> "When I blow I think of times and things from outa the past that gives me an image . . . a town, a chick somewhere back down the line, an old man with no name you once seen in a place you don't remember. What you hear coming from a man's horn, that's what he is. . . ."

CHAPTER 9

BIX AND THE ROARING TWENTIES

The Jazz Age in America began during the First World War with the appearance of the Original Dixieland Jass Band in New York, and it ended with the stock market crash in 1929. This was one of the most unusual and frenzied periods in American history. Hot jazz was king during the Roaring Twenties, the decade of the flapper, silent movies, prohibition, bathtub gin, and the Charleston.

In some respects the twenties resemble the sixties: the country was riding the crest of prosperity, the younger generation was turning its back on the Victorianism of an earlier America and shaping its own "new" morality. A social revolution was in progress—women had gained the right to vote, shortened their skirts and smoked cigarettes. Then, as now, popular dances required the physical exertion of youth. They danced the Charleston to the driving beat of hot jazz; drank bootleg [illegal] gin from hip flasks and drove the sports car of that day, the Stutz Bearcat.

Into this chaotic era stepped a round-faced young man from the Midwest, carrying a stubby cornet under his arm. His name was Bix Beiderbecke [rhymes with wider check] and it was his destiny not to outlive the age he typified. So great was the legend of Beiderbecke that his meteoric rise and tragic life inspired Dorothy Baker to write the novel *Young Man with a Horn.*

Bix was perfect material, a sensitive, good-looking, young man with one obsession in life—he lived for his horn, always searching for that perfect note. His life story was ideal for the pages of a novel—after-hour jam sessions in hotel rooms and smoky cellars, colorful characters, gallons of bathtub gin and, always, hot jazz.

In his brief career, Bix rose to sparkling heights, the idol of jazz followers. He was riding the crest of his fame when the stock market crashed. By then, Bix's health was shot; and soon after he started down a toboggan slide professionally. Too much prohibition gin and too little sleep had weakened him, and he caught a summer cold which quickly turned into pneumonia. He was twenty-eight when he died in 1931.

Bix Beiderbecke and Louis Armstrong were the great cornet men of the twenties. They admired one another tremendously, and the two of them probably had as much influence on jazz music as any two men who lived, yet their playing was not at all alike. Louis' solos were dramatic and uninhibited. Bix, on the other hand, despite his drive, played with a curious restraint. His solos gave one the feeling of a volcano which might erupt any second but for the lid he held down tightly. Now and then one of his explosive rips would let off some of the steam.

Bix played with an outstanding purity and roundness of tone that was his trademark. Hoagy Carmichael says the notes came out of Bix's horn like chimes struck with a mallet.

Musicians who knew Bix in those days flounder for words to express his effect on them both musically and as a person. *A History of Jazz in America* quotes Paul Whiteman, in whose orchestra Bix was a shining star:

> "Bix was not only the greatest musician I've ever known but also the greatest gentleman I've ever known . . . Somehow or other he gave you the impression that he was constantly striving for something that was just out of reach . . . And I just can't describe that tone, those notes and phrases, and least of all, the feeling with which he played. To me, there's never been a soloist like him, and let me tell you, I'd give my right arm if I could live to hear another Bix. I think my arm's safe, though!"

Leon Bismarck "Bix" Beiderbecke was born in Davenport, Iowa on March 10, 1903. Bix grew up in musical surroundings that were quite different from those Louis Armstrong knew in his youth. Bix's German-American family was in the lumber business. In this upper middle-class environment, Bix was given piano lessons at an early age. His family hoped he might become a concert pianist. The lessons must not have been very extensive however, because Bix was never known to win any prizes at reading music. And although he later became as well known a jazz pianist as cornetist, some musicians who played with him say he could play piano only in the key of C.

It was in high school that Bix decided he wanted to play the cornet. He asked his uncle Al Peterson, a local bandleader and cornet player, for some lessons. Uncle Al, however, didn't think Bix was serious and put him off. Bix shrugged, went out and bought himself a cornet, and the next time Uncle Al came to the house, he was astonished to hear the boy playing popular tunes on the horn. The fact that Bix was self-taught showed up in his later playing. Musicians who played with him noticed he used an unorthodox style of fingering. His lack of reading ability got him into professional hot water on many occasions. But none of these technical shortcomings detracted from the extraordinary beauty of his playing.

While in high school, Bix played on a truck with a high-school jazz band at football games, and he sat in with bands around his hometown. His biggest thrill came from going down to the river to listen to the bands that played on the riverboats. Here, as a teen-ager, he heard authentic New Orleans jazz played by Louis Armstrong, Kid Ory and Johnny and Baby Dodds.

Some jazz historians say that Bix got his idea of pure cornet tone from Emmett Hardy, a riverboat cornet man. It seems though, from his records, that Bix was more influenced by the sounds of the Original Dixieland Jass Band whose early records he memorized. This band had a push and drive that became characteristic of Bix's best playing.

Many great Negro jazzman of that time including King Oliver and Louis Armstrong flavored their New Orleans jazz with a blues element that set it apart from the drive of the Original Dixieland Jass Band. Speaking in a technical sense, if one is striving to draw a fine line between the various styles and schools of jazz, which is difficult, Bix could have been classed more a Dixieland cornetist than Louis Armstrong, who is in a class by himself.

To draw the line even finer, Bix was one of the young, white, mid-western jazzmen of the 1920's who played Chicago-style jazz. This style grew from the style of the Original Dixieland Jazz Band but developed distinct differences. It got away from the parade-band sound of 2/4 time and usually had four strong beats to the measure. Chicago jazz probably has the most intense, driving undercurrent of rhythm of all jazz styles. Also, these mid-western jazzmen began using an instrument foreign to the New Orleans bands—the tenor saxophone.

When Bix graduated from high school, he went on to the Lake Forest Academy in Chicago where he displayed more interest in slipping off downtown to play with jazz musicians than he did in the school's curriculum. He left school after a year, and the next summer got his first professional music job on a Lake Michigan excursion boat. In the band was a Jewish boy, still in short pants, playing clarinet. He was to become the "King of Swing" in the big-band days of the 1930's. His name was Benny Goodman.

Bix and some of the other musicians who played on the excursion boat then joined a group called the Wolverines which was founded by the pianist Dick Voynow. They used the instrumentation of the New Orleans jazz bands with the addition of the tenor saxophone. The group became quite popular in the Midwest, playing in theaters, dance halls and ballrooms and for university dances. These were the days when the bloody, prohibition gang wars were beginning. Like Louis, Bix found out what it was like to play his horn while dodging bullets. The Wolverines were playing at the Stockton Club on New Year's Eve, 1923, when a fight broke out among some bootleggers who were present. With the sounds of pistol shots, crashing furniture and splintering glassware for a background, the Wolverines launched into a fast and furious version of "China Boy" that lasted over an hour. Bix, who was usually off in a world of his own anyway, leaned back and played a succession of rousing jazz solos, oblivious of the disturbance.

It was with the Wolverine band that Bix made his first recordings, "Jazz Me Blues," "Fidgety Feet," "Oh, Baby," "Copenhagen," "Riverboat Shuffle," "Susie," "I Need Some Pettin'," "Tiger Rag" and "Royal Garden Blues." These records were made in 1924, under primitive conditions, at a time when the recording industry was in its infancy. The recording quality is extremely poor compared to today's methods. This is especially tragic because Bix did not live long enough to record on equipment which would have given us a more realistic reproduction of his beautiful, pure tone. Our appreciation of him will forever be limited by the thin, somewhat tinny sound on those discs which musicians who heard Bix say don't do him justice. Bix must have blown up quite a storm in person, because, even with the limitations of these early-day records, he sounds very good coming to us from across the decades.

Bix's professional musical activities took place mostly in the Chicago area and in New York. In the summer of 1925, Bix got a job with Frank Trumbauer's band. Trumbauer, who played C-melody sax, became one of Bix's closest musical associates and they made many records together. In 1926, both Trumbauer and Bix were hired by Gene Goldkette, whose orchestra was one of the leading jazz groups in the country.

During his entire, short adult life, Bix was totally immersed in his music. He had little interest in anything material. We can see him now, finishing a music engagement at a college prom where co-eds in short, fringed skirts have been dancing the Charleston to his jazz. It is two in the morning, but for Bix and his friends the evening has just started. They pile into a Stutz Bearcat and roar off to a speakeasy where a jam session is going on. In the smoky, dimly lit cellar, Bix takes his horn out of its case. Somebody hands him a bottle of bootleg gin. Then the piano and drums start playing and Bix raises his horn to his lips. His face contorts with concentrated effort as the driving notes spill from his horn. At five o'clock, the crowd adjourns to a hotel where a party is in progress. A charge of excitement churns the room. Bix is here. He is rushed to the piano. By now his body is aching with fatigue, but more bathtub gin will fix that. The air is dense with heavy layers of cigarette smoke. The crowd around the piano is four deep as Bix plays; outside, dawn is lighting the city's rooftops, but Bix plays on. Finally the party ends. The young musician flops on a couch, fully clothed, and drops off to sleep. But in a few hours he will be at another jam session still trying to hit that perfect note.

In a sense, Bix was one of the young rebels of his generation. He turned his back on a career as a concert pianist, or any profitable business his family background could have given him, to seek his identity and answer in the music of his day.

Close musician friends of Bix, such as Frank Trumbauer, Eddie Condon and Jimmy McPartland, have described him as something of an intellectual with a great interest in modern classical composers as well as in jazz. Bix's favorite composers were Debussy, Stravinsky, Cyril Scott, Eastwood Lane, Schoenberg and Ravel. Bix's exquisitely haunting piano compositions, "In a Mist," "By Candlelight," "Flashes," and "In the Dark" reflect the influence of the Impressionist composers.

Bix was far ahead of his time, striving for new horizons in jazz that were not to be reached for another two decades when bop, cool jazz and progressive jazz came on the scene. Make no mistake, Bix played hot jazz, but there was a foreshadowing in his musical thinking of new areas of jazz expression, more complex chord alterations and whole-tone scale experiments. In his jazz solos, Bix chose his notes carefully, playing with taste and meaning rather than merely playing a great quantity of fast notes to show off technical skill.

Bix was a typical absentminded genius. Eddie Condon, in his book *We Called it Music,* recalls that Bix was forever forgetting where he'd put his cornet and then stepping on it. He ran through any number of cornets for this reason. Often, when Bix came into town on a music job he had overlooked such mundane considerations as clothes. His friends had to hustle around and borrow a tuxedo for him. Bix, always good-natured and affable, would thank everyone and wander off to his playing job, cornet under his arm, his head in the clouds. He might show up a few days later in another tuxedo without remembering where it came from.

Eddie Condon also tells how Bix and clarinetist Pee Wee Russell shared a lake cottage while playing with a Gene Goldkette unit at a summer resort. After a few weeks of habitation by the two musicians, the cottage looked like a disaster area. The floors had disappeared beneath a tide of empty gin bottles, sheet music, sardine cans and discarded clarinet reeds. Bix and Pee Wee had ordered milk delivered to the cottage, but they kept forgetting to bring it in, so the bottles piled up on the back porch. During the course of the summer, Bix and Pee Wee decided to buy a car. They trustingly allowed a dealer to sell them an ancient Buick. After one brief trip of a few blocks the car shuddered and gave up the ghost. They pushed it home where it sat in the backyard near the growing stack of unopened milk bottles. The car wasn't a total loss, however—for the remainder of the summer, Bix and Pee Wee used the rearview mirror for shaving.

Bix's good nature was partly responsible for his downfall. He did not know how to say no. During the height of his fame, he was denied any privacy or time to rest. His fans would bang on his hotel room door at three, four or five in the morning, wanting to hear him play; and Bix, too obliging to turn anyone down, would drag himself out of bed and soon there would be another party going on in his room. Eventually, the constant lack of sleep, erratic hours and consumption of bootleg gin undermined Bix's health.

Gene Goldkette's band, which Bix had joined in 1926, broke up in 1927 and Bix went on to the big Paul Whiteman orchestra. Bix's individuality was submerged in its pretentious arrangements. He played best in small groups. Not being a very good sight reader, Bix had to work hard to keep up with the complex scores. Nevertheless, Whiteman recognized Bix's greatness and featured his solo work as much as possible. Whiteman was a generous man to work for. He paid Bix three hundred dollars a week, which would amount to many times that much in today's devalued dollars. And in 1929, when Bix's health began to fail, Whiteman sent him off for a year's rest, keeping him on full salary the entire time.

Bix came back from his vacation as round-faced and likeable as ever, but he never fully recovered his health. His cornet playing became ragged and unreliable. He left Whiteman's band and tried to get odd jobs playing for radio shows, but these jobs required considerable sight-reading and Bix wasn't fast enough at it. By the spring of 1931 his health was so bad he couldn't be relied on as a cornet player. To some musicians, the fallen jazz idol had become a freak. In an awed voice they would say, "I played on a job with Bix last week and, man, you couldn't believe how terrible he was. He was cracking and missing notes all over the place—"

Those final months, Bix had a piano in his room in the Forty-fourth Street Hotel in New York. His cornet playing might have gone to the dogs, but he could still play the piano using those strange, way-out chords that fascinated everyone who heard them. Almost every night there was a drunken party going on in Bix's room, which was crowded with musicians and celebrities who came to hear him improvise on the piano.

Bix spent a lot of those final months working on his piano compositions. He couldn't write music well enough to score his own compositions, but arranger and composer friends obligingly put them on paper for him. Bix seemed to sense that his time was limited and he wanted to leave his piano compositions as a record of his playing.

That summer, Bix came down with a bad cold. His body, weakened from the years of dissipation, irregular hours and heavy drinking, couldn't throw it off. The cold turned into pneumonia and Bix died on August 7, 1931, at the age of twenty-eight.

Some jazz critics say that so much legend has grown up around Bix's life that his importance as a jazz musician is overrated, while others maintain he was one of the greatest jazzmen of all times. Whichever the case, Bix's life is important because it so typifies the music of his generation.

Bix made many recordings while with Paul Whiteman and Gene Goldkette, but the recordings for which he is best known were made with a small group of his own and with Frank Trumbauer's small jazz unit. They include such titles as "Singin' the Blues," which has one of his best known solos, "Way Down Yonder in New Orleans" and "For No Reason at All in C," on which Bix played both cornet and piano. On "Sorry" and "Since My Best Gal Turned Me Down," Bix played the Dixieland style he liked best. Perhaps his most touching and best remembered recording is his own piano rendition of his composition "In a Mist." The title pretty well describes his life.

CHAPTER 10

PAUL WHITEMAN MAKES A LADY OUT OF JAZZ

It is February 12, 1924. A concert hall in New York City is filled with an expectant crowd. Among the faces are the leading composers and music critics of the day. They have come to hear a most unusual concert.

In the audience, a symphony conductor taking a busman's holiday glances around the room and then turns to his companion. "I never thought I'd hear a concert of popular music in Aeolian Hall. Nothing but classical music has been played here before. These walls are sacred."

His friend nods. "It's the times, I suppose. They say we are living in the jazz age. I must confess I don't really know what jazz music is; do you?"

The conductor dismisses the subject with an impatient wave of his hand. "Jazz—it isn't music. It's noise. Untrained musicians making sounds on their instruments like braying animals. It's a novelty—a fad."

"And yet we've come to a jazz concert."

"I came out of curiosity. If anyone can pull off a stunt

like this, it's Paul Whiteman. The man is an excellent musician as well as a flamboyant showman."

"I would say he has attracted some notable people tonight for whatever he has in mind. I have seen Damrosch, Heifetz, Kreisler, McCormack, Rachmaninov, Rosenthal [Moriz] and Stokowski in the audience."

"Yes, yes—they're all here. Music critics and writers, too. There's Deems Taylor . . . no, over there in the next row. I suppose they're here for the same reason I am—curiosity. I particularly want to hear this new composition "Rhapsody in Blue." The composer, that young fellow George Gershwin, is going to play it. I understand he's attempted to join the jazz element with the concert form. Should be interesting."

On the stage, the conductor strides to the podium. He is a commanding figure, a tall man, well known to the world of popular music, Paul Whiteman. He raises his baton and in the fleeting moment before he brings it down, many thoughts race through his mind. The months of planning and work that have gone into this jazz concert. The financial gamble—expenses over eleven thousand dollars. But more than money, the artistic risk. Suppose the critics sneer at tonight's unusual concert. It could be disastrous to the public's acceptance of jazz and popular music.

Whiteman knew the difficulties involved. He had recognized the impact of the Original Dixieland Jass Band on popular music. But jazz was the music of honky-tonks and gangsters' speakeasies. How could it be presented in a manner acceptable to polite society and the formidable critics?

And yet he felt confident they would accept jazz on his terms. No brash sounds, no unrestrained improvisation. His orchestra was big and smooth, with every note they played written and rehearsed until it was like a polished gem. He wasn't leading a five-piece street band. His orchestra filled the stage, impressive by sheer numbers and the battery of instruments at hand—celesta, flugelhorn, basset horn, heckelphone and euphonium in addition to less exotic brass, reed and stringed instruments.

He had preceded the concert with a gigantic publicity compaign. Music critics had been entertained at lunch and admitted to rehearsals. It had been explained to them, as Whiteman later wrote in *Jazz,* that he hoped the concert would prove "the advance which has been made in popular music from the day of discordant jazz to the melodious form of the present. . . ."

And now it was time to test his theory. He brought down his baton. The orchestra began with a suite of four serenades written especially for the concert, then they played dance versions of "The Volga Boatman" and "To a Wild Rose." Tin Pan Alley favorites such as "Whispering," "Limehouse Blues," "Alexander's Ragtime Band" and "A Pretty Girl is Like a Melody" were given the full Paul Whiteman treatment. And the climax of the concert came when George Gershwin played "Rhapsody in Blue" with the orchestra.

The concert was a critical if not a financial success. Whiteman lost seven thousand dollars on the event, but he felt it was money well spent considering the far-reaching benefits to popular music. The audience applauded the concert enthusiastically for Whiteman had presented jazz in such a way as to shock no one. He used European concert devices and blended them with jazz.

If a New Orleans jazz musician had seen "jazz" in an advertisement of the event that night and had wandered into the hall, he would certainly have felt he was in the wrong place. There was none of the free-wheeling improvisation, the unfettered individual inspiration, the pulsing beat of jazz. And yet, the concert at Aeolian Hall that February night in 1924 was a milestone in the development of jazz music. It had lasting effects on all jazz musicians. After Whiteman's epic concert, jazz was no longer a dirty word. Music critics and the press began to regard it as a serious art form and worthy of attention. The taint of disrespectability was fading. Jazz musicians found it easier to get work. Out of the concert grew the well-known phrase, "Paul Whiteman made a lady out of jazz."

Whiteman towered over the jazz world during the 1920's like a majestic musical father. To the musicians who fell under his benevolent shadow, he was fondly known as "Pops" or "Fatho." To the general public he was "The King of Jazz." Through the ranks of his orchestra passed such jazzmen as Frankie Trumbauer, Red Norvo, Bix Beiderbecke, Tommy and Jimmy Dorsey, Eddie Lang, Joe Venuti and the "old groaner" himself, Bing Crosby.

Ironically, Whiteman's orchestra did not play true jazz, though he often featured brief, hot solos by the jazzmen buried somewhere in the tiers of violins, cellos and oboes. His orchestra leaned more to semi-symphonic treatment of popular music than to swinging call and response patterns, moving rhythms and freer improvisations.

Whiteman was one of the hugely successful commercial bandleaders who wisely had his finger on the public pulse. Born in Denver, Colorado, in 1890, he started as a violinist. By 1922 he controlled twenty-eight bands playing on the East Coast and was said to gross over a million dollars a year. In 1930, he was starred in one of the first all-talking movies "The King of Jazz." His was one of the featured musical organizations in the early days of radio.

There were other band leaders in the 1920's who were making a commercial success in the popular music field, though the music they played was not true jazz. Among the popular dance bands of that era were Ben Bernie, Isham Jones, Hal Kemp, Jan Garber and Ted Weems. Guy Lombardo with his Royal Canadians has been playing "The Sweetest Music This Side of Heaven," and making a fortune at it, since the 1920's.

The music these groups played grew more directly out of the traditions of ragtime, vaudeville, musical comedy, Strauss waltzes and Tin Pan Alley ballads than from New Orleans jazz, although they reflected a certain watered-down jazz influence. Some of the feeling of jazz rhythm can be found in their music, though there is little room for improvisation in their arrangements and their rhythm is designed primarily for dancing the businessman's bounce or as a polite dining background. The arrangements were often marked by repeated gimmicks or musical clichés which musicians call "Mickey Mouse." They presented the melody in easily recognizable fashion and include polkas, schottisches, waltzes and Latin rhythm dances in their programs. Because their music was specifically designed and packaged for the taste of the buying public, it was called commercial. The artistic content may have been slight, but it did serve a purpose in the area of entertainment and in the field of popular music.

CHAPTER 11

THE AUSTIN HIGH GANG AND CHICAGO JAZZ

While Paul Whiteman was busily selling a palatable version of jazz to the public on a grand scale, a group of high-school boys from Austin, an upper middle-class suburb of Chicago, were about to make a historic contribution to the real thing.

These boys who attended Austin High were the intellectuals and rebels of their set. They read *The American Mercury* magazine, in whose pages social critics like H. L. Mencken and George Jean Nathan lambasted the pillars of the community and the hypocrisy of the Establishment. The Austin High boys did their social protesting with their own style of firebrand jazz.

Austin was a town of tall shade trees, spacious, clipped lawns and fine, sedate houses. Monotonous respectability hung over the suburb like smog. Music, to the staid citizens of the area, had to be polite and sugary—muted violins, timid saxophones, tinkling pianos. Jazz was considered trashy noise.

But the Austin High gang, whose ringleader was a skinny kid wearing thick glasses, Frank Teschemacher, had other ideas. After school, the gang got together at Frank's house and listened avidly to recordings by the New Orleans Rhythm Kings. It was a new voice speaking to them, this smoky, gutsy, down-to-earth folk music called jazz that had rolled up the Mississippi from the deep South. It was a breath of new life in their buttoned-down environment.

In the evenings, the Austin High gang—Jimmy McPartland and his brother Dick, Dave North, Jimmy Lanigan and Bud Freeman, with Frank Teschemacher ("Tesch" for short) in the lead—cruised around Chicago gulping down a rich diet of live jazz. They were in the right town for it; because in the early 1920's, Chicago was jumping with fine jazz. The boys studied the grace of New Orleans Negro clarinetists Jimmie Noone and Johnny Dodds. The story is told that when Jimmie Noone played at the Apex Club in Chicago, composer Maurice Ravel, accompanied by members of the Chicago symphony, went to listen with amazement to his clarinet playing.

Those were electric years for jazz in Chicago, the years King Oliver played at the Lincoln Gardens and sent for Louis Armstrong. The Austin High boys, still in knee britches, sopped up those fine jazz sounds like a hungry blotter going after spilled ink. In their trips of musical exploration, the Austin kids met other jazz-hungry youngsters who, like themselves, were haunting the music spots of Chicago: Floyd O'Brien, Muggsy Spanier, Eddie Condon, Gene Krupa, Joe Sullivan, Benny Goodman—all future jazz greats. And they heard the up-and-coming musicians who were already playing professionally, Bix Beiderbecke, Joe Marsala, Wild Bill Davidson, Jack Teagarden, Jess Stacy and Pee Wee Russell.

The Austin High kids all played violin—most youngsters in those days were given a dose of culture in the form of violin lessons whether they liked it or not—but their enthusiasm for jazz was making them eye other instruments. Their hangout was a drugstore called the Spoon and Straw which was located just across the street from school. They were there one afternoon when Frank Teschemacher announced, "I've been practicing with a clarinet. I've got 'Clarinet Marmalade' down pretty good."

"I can't make up my mind if I want to be a drummer or a tap dancer," Bud Freeman said.

"Listen," Tesch said excitedly, "why don't we try to work something out together? Dave North can play piano. We could copy those New Orleans Rhythm King records. It would be the cat's pajamas."

"Maybe I could play drums," Bud Freeman offered.

One of the group knew a kid named Dave Tough over at the Lewis Institute who was interested in jazz. They went to see him. Dave was a drummer. When he got through giving them a demonstration, Bud said, "Maybe I ought to start on something besides drums." Dave told him, "I know where you can get a C-melody sax."

So, the band of the Austin High kids was born. Bud Freeman honked and struggled with the C-melody saxophone, eventually switching to tenor sax. Tesch squeeked on the clarinet. But something in their group, a vitality and enthusiasm, gave their jazz a fresh power and drive not heard before. They played in the Dixieland style, but felt hampered by the traditional 2/4 beat. They gradually changed to a steadier, driving, solid four beats to the measure. Their notes came out like smouldering coals.

Tesch was the generating force in the group. When he played, he tried to blow himself through his horn. His notes flew like sparks struck from a piece of flint. He was not a polished clarinet player; occasionally, in his excitement, his fingers got tangled up and he hit some clinkers. But he can be forgiven when one feels the excitement he brought to the records made by the Austin High bunch. When Tesch played, it was like plugging the whole band into an electrical outlet and turning a switch on.

The gang was going pretty well by 1924 and started playing some professional jobs, first under the name of the Blue Friars. In the summer of that year they played at a resort on Lake Lost, not far from the city. The next fall they broadcast over one of Chicago's pioneer radio stations WHT, under the name of O'Hare's Red Dragons; O'Hare was a promoter who got them the job.

For the next several years, the Austin High kids played in and around Chicago, earning themselves a jazz reputation. Milton "Mezz" Mezzrow, who played with the group from time to time, became a friend of their ringleader Tesch. In his book *Really the Blues,* Mezzrow describes Tesch as a studious kid inclined to be pessimistic. About the future of their music, Tesch once told Mezzrow:

> "What's the use, Milton? You knock yourself out making great new music for the people and they treat you like some kind of plague or blight, like you were offering them leprosy instead of art, and you wind up in the poor house or the asylum. That's the way it always goes with a real artist who won't put his talents on the auction block to be sold to the highest bidder."

Tesch was voicing the frustrations many jazzmen feel when they watch the general public go ape over some commercial gimmick or trite novelty, while ignoring the true jazz artists.

Mezzrow relates how he and Tesch drove around in Mezzrow's car one night and stopped in Chicago's Grant Park where they took out their clarinets and played jazz duets to the stars. Suddenly, a motorcycle policeman appeared. Tesch, always the pessimist, blinked like a somber owl behind his thick glasses and predicted the worst. He knew that conventional society would have difficulty understanding why a pair of jazz musicians would find a poetic logic in playing a serenade in a touring car in a public park at three o'clock in the morning.

The boys awaited their fate as the cop strode up to the car. He looked them over, then to their amazement said, "That's the best music I've heard in a long time, boys. Keep it up."

From then on, when the gang was in the mood for an open-air jam session, they piled as many musicians as possible into Mezzrow's car and went to the park where they played until the sun came up.

In 1927, Tesch and his buddies came under the influence of a patron Charles Pierce, a South Side butcher. He was an unusual man to be a benefactor of the arts, but he loved jazz and used the money he made from the meat business to promote and help jazz musicians. He set up the first recording date for Tesch and his crowd in October, 1927. During the next few years they had a number of recording sessions. Their records have been assembled in a collectors' album reissued by Brunswick, entitled *Tesch, Chicago Style Clarinetist.* These discs contain some of the best Chicago-style jazz ever recorded. The young musicians who made the records with Tesch included Muggsy Spanier (trumpet), Wingy Manone (trumpet), Red McKenzie (vocal), Eddie Condon (banjo), Gene Krupa (drums), George Wettling (drums), Mess Mezzrow (clarinet and saxophone), Bud Freeman (saxophone), Joe Sullivan (piano) and Art Hodes (piano).

During the recording of one of the numbers in the collection "There'll Be Some Changes Made," which incidentally is one of the best recordings made by the group, an event occurred which later appeared as a fictionalized incident in *Young Man with a Horn.* In the novel Rick, the protagonist, has started going downhill. In a dramatic scene, he is playing a jazz solo and reaches for a high note that isn't there—he's too far gone to blow it. He rushes over and throws his horn out of the window. What actually took place during the recording of "Changes" was that Muggsy Spanier, playing trumpet, missed the last note completely. Furious with himself, he tried to throw his horn out of the window, but the rest of the group stopped him. He was all for destroying the recording and making it over; but when it was played back, the band knew they were listening to a jazz masterpiece. The spontaneous fire and drive could never be duplicated, so the record was issued as it was. As long as jazz fans play that recording, Muggsy will go on missing the final note.

Tesch sparkles on all these records which were made at a time when the recording industry was hitting its stride. From the first records made by the Original Dixieland Jass Band in 1917 to those of the Austin High gang in 1927, record-making had grown into a gigantic industry. In 1926, over a hundred and fifty million records were sold in America. Records had a great deal to do with the spread of jazz. The ten-inch 78 rpm discs, with all their scratchiness and lack of true fidelity, spread the gospel of jazz to isolated corners of America and Europe, far from the jazz meccas of Chicago and New York.

But while the record industry was prospering, a new fad was sweeping the nation—radio. It was to have its own far-reaching effects on jazz. In every town across the country, radio bugs were sitting up late at night fiddling with crystal sets, straining at earphones hoping to pick up something on the airwaves. What they heard—when they got anything—was apt to be live music played late at night in hotels in Chicago, New York, St. Louis and other major cities. In the early days of radio, this live music was the backbone of radio programming.

The Austin High boys knew the taste of fame when their records came out. But styles in music change quickly, and the public's taste is fickle. The stock market crash in 1929 marked a declining public interest in Chicago-style jazz. The trend was to sweet, Guy Lombardo-type music and bigger, smoother bands.

Tesch was reduced to playing in some of the Mickey Mouse, commercial bands. He made a few more jazz recordings, but was destined to outlive his contemporary Bix, by only a few months. One cold night in January, 1932, he was riding to a job with Wild Bill Davison. The car skidded, Tesch was thrown out, and he died at the age of twenty-seven on an icy Chicago street. It was too bad, really, because he was just getting the hang of playing the clarinet.

CHAPTER 12

JAZZ IMPROVISATION

To the uninitiated, a jazz ensemble produces a strange mixture of sounds, with each musician in the band frequently going off on a wild tangent of his own. The usual reaction is a plaintive, "But where's the melody?" The listener may find his toe tapping to a provocative, rhythmic undercurrent and he may even discover his emotions responding to an indefinable something in the music; but from an intellectual standpoint, he hasn't the vaguest idea what is taking place.

What was Bix doing when he played his immortal jazz? How did Louis Armstrong stray from the melody line and create his original phrases? What is it that Pete Fountain, Al Hirt, Benny Goodman, Dizzy Gillespie, Miles Davis and all the others, well known or obscure, do that sets their music apart and makes it jazz?

Two elements are at the heart of jazz—the beat and improvisation. The beat is the foundation which grew out of African drumbeats, handclapping spirituals and parade music—the rhythm that makes feet tap and stirs the emotion, the pulse that makes one want to dance.

MINSTRELS—A popular form of stage entertainment of the late 19th century which helped spread the sound of Negro slave music to the outside world. (Photo courtesy Library of Congress)

THE ORIGINAL DIXIELAND "JASS" BAND—Tony Sbarbaro (Drums), Eddie Edwards (Trombone), "Nick" La Rocca (Cornet), Larry Shields (Clarinet), and Harry Ragas (Piano). (Photo courtesy RCA Victor Records)

AN EARLY RECORDING SESSION—Note how closely the musicians are grouped around the "recording horn" which was used before the development of the modern microphone. It was on such equipment that the early jazz musicians recorded; thus much of the true quality of their tone has been lost. (Photo courtesy RCA Victor Records)

"KING" OLIVER—The leader of the first Negro jazz band to make jazz records; Louis Armstrong's teacher and inspiration. (Photo courtesy RCA Victor Records)

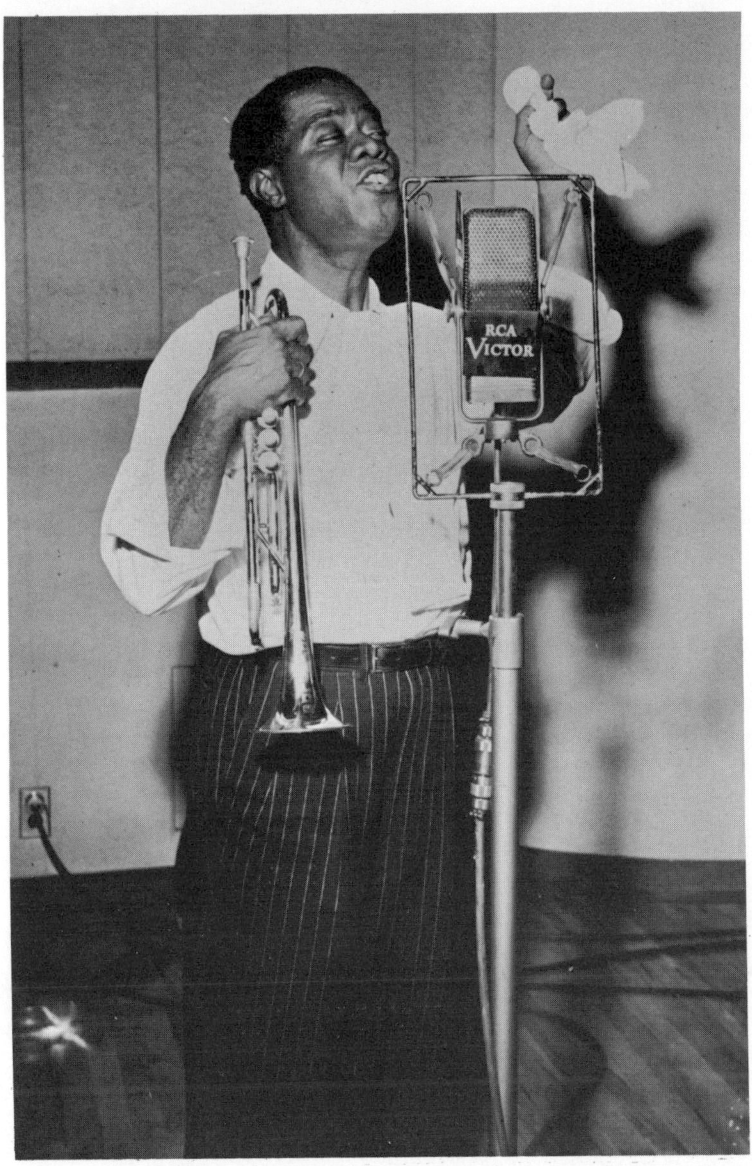

LOUIS "SATCHMO" ARMSTRONG—(Photo courtesy RCA Victor Records)

BIX BEIDERBECKE—"The Young Man With a Horn." His short, tragic life became one of the legends of the jazz age. (Photo courtesy RCA Victor Records)

PAUL WHITEMAN AND HIS ORCHESTRA—(Photo courtesy RCA Victor Records)

BENNY GOODMAN—Shown outside the Kremlin during his tour of the Soviet Union. (Photo courtesy RCA Victor Records)

FATS WALLER—Jazz pianist and composer, noted for his powerful "stride" bass style. (Photo courtesy RCA Victor Records)

COLEMAN HAWKINS ("The Hawk")—His recording of "Body And Soul" in the 1930's was a masterpiece and became a model for aspiring tenor sax men. (Photo courtesy RCA Victor Records)

COUNT BASIE

EDWARD KENNEDY "DUKE" ELLINGTON—Jazz pianist, composer, and arranger. (Photo courtesy RCA Victor Records)

Improvisation, as already stated, means extemporaneous musical invention. But the jazzman does not merely play a hodge-podge of meaningless notes. His improvisation, or jazz solo, bears a certain relationship to the original melody—it follows the melody's chord progression. This is not quite as easily explainable as rhythm, for to understand it one must delve a bit into the basic structure of music.

Now, the music of our Western culture makes sense to our ears because it follows a musical scale we are accustomed to hearing, just as our language is based on a certain alphabet. Oriental music sounds weird to us because it is based upon a scale entirely different from our own. Think how mixed-up we would become if suddenly our alphabet had, say, forty-nine letters instead of only twenty-six.

Our musical scale was originally comprised of five notes. For a demonstration of this simple, "pentatonic" scale, sing the tones of the present major scale—but leave out fa and ti. The pentatonic scale may be demonstrated on the piano by playing the five black keys in a row, beginning with G flat. This grouping of three then two black keys automatically produces the proper intervals of the pentatonic scale. This five-tone scale was used by the Greeks and by the early Christian church. It was also the scale familiar to the Africans before they were enslaved and brought to America.

Back in the eleventh century there lived a Benedictine monk called Guido d'Arezzo (about 990 to 1050) who was a music reformer and innovator. In his day, all serious music was church music, and it was based on music forms borrowed from the Greeks. Since Guido lived so long ago and time has obscured many facts, we can't be positive that he did all the things he has been given credit for. But it was Guido, or some person or persons who lived about his time, who added two notes to the five-tone scale. By doing this he could produce more interesting and varied musical effects. What he came up with was the seven-tone scale we use today (the eighth note is the first repeated an octave higher).

The fourth and seventh tones (fa and ti) were the ones added by Guido or his contemporaries, and the result is what we call the "diatonic" scale. On the piano, you can play this scale in the key of C by beginning at *c* and playing the seven white keys that follow, winding up on the eighth an octave higher.

When old Guido got to swinging with this new scale, he was something of a progressive. The Greeks hadn't known what harmony was, but using the diatonic scale, choirs produced pleasing harmony by singing notes a third apart, for example: do, mi and sol. This is the basic major chord.

By beginning on the fourth note of the scale, fa, and building a chord in the same manner, the early Christian composers came up with a related chord called the sub-dominant: fa, la and do from the second octave.

With very simple chords like these, medieval Christian composers produced their chants and hymns. But our musical language, like our spoken language, is constantly changing. The English of Chaucer's day would sound like a foreign tongue to us now; and our music has grown much more sophisticated and complicated, too.

In the seventeenth century, an Italian composer Monteverdi (1567–1643) decided to improve upon the music of his time with some new sounds. Long before Monteverdi came along, it had been noticed that Guido's seventh note, ti, just naturally led, or resolved, into the eighth, do. In other words, if you run up the scale and stop on ti you feel dissatisfied. The scale is incomplete. Stopping on ti gives you an anxious feeling, musically speaking, and you want to sing do to complete the musical experience. For this reason, ti came to be known as the leading tone—it led back to home base, the starting note of the scale.

Monteverdi decided to capitalize on the idea and invent a chord to intensify the leading tone. It was constructed from the fifth and seventh notes of the scale combined with the second and fourth notes from the octave above it. Monteverdi's chord, called the "dominant" or "dominant seventh," hangs in the air like a question needing an answer. If we follow it with the major chord, we feel satisfied. The musical psychology of the dominant seventh resolving into its major chord is one of the most moving forces in our music. The chord so revolutionized the music of Monteverdi's day that there were some dark mutterings among other musicians about having him chased out of town. People who have new ideas often find themselves in this kind of hot water.

With the introduction of the dominant seventh chord, our music had three interesting chords on which to build melodies: the major chord based on the tonic or first note of the scale, the sub-dominant based on the fourth note and the dominant seventh based on the fifth note. These related chords have a beautiful way of resolving one into another; this is called "chord progression." Most of our church music, simple folk ballads, rock 'n' roll and blues are based on these three chords.

Now, musical compositions are melodies accompanied by a series of chord progressions played in the same key. A musician knows that he can play other notes beside those in the melody and they will not sound wrong or out of tune as long as they follow the scale of the underlying chords. To the jazzman, no law says he has to stick to the notes of the melody or play them exactly as written. There are seven notes in the scale, and they can all be played without clashing with the melody. In his improvisations, an advanced jazzman who knows what he is doing might even put in still other half-tones and use substitute and altered chords.

Given the proper rhythm, any tune can be turned into a hot jump tune or a cool jazz number. The jazz performer might play the melody once or twice in rhythmic style as it is written, then he might embark on several choruses in different variations all based upon the original progression of the underlying chords.

We have tried to analyze some of the technique of playing jazz, but the difficulty is that jazz is so spontaneous and personal that it defies strict analysis. A jazz solo cannot be written so it can be reproduced exactly as it was originally played. An arranger once copied, note for note, a recording made by Bix Beiderbecke. Later Bix was given the music and asked to play it. He got through the ensemble part, but when he came to his solo, he stopped. He couldn't read the notes he had composed himself in his extemporaneous solo!

The difficulty comes from the slurs, tonal qualities, subtle rhythms and polyrhythms in jazz that cannot be captured on paper. Arrangements for a symphonic orchestra can be scored; but it is a jazz axiom that real jazz cannot be written, it must be played and listened to.

CHAPTER 13

ONE-NIGHT STANDS

Much of the jazz being played during prohibition was heard in speakeasies in the larger cities. But there was another vast market for popular music and that was the dance halls and ballrooms scattered throughout the country in smaller towns. In the early 1920's, dance bands realized the great potential demand for their music, and many bands went on the road. Thus, territory bands and one-night stands were born.

When a name band came to town, dancers crowded around the bandstand to see the famous musicians in action. To the fans, the life of the bandleader and the professional musician was filled with glamour, almost equal to being a movie star. The fans saw the sharp tuxedos and spats and the gleaming instruments, and thought how great it would be just to travel around playing music for a living.

What the fans did not see were the long, exhausting drives between jobs, the way the musicians slept and lived in a crowded touring car or bus, never having time to have their laundry done properly, grabbing what meals they could at irregular hours, battling car trouble and primitive roads while rushing through the night.

This was long before our superhighways. In fact, most roads were not even paved or graveled. Many of them were simply rutted dirt lanes. Service stations were few and far between. A flat tire meant taking the tire off the rim—on the side of the road in the weeds—removing the tube, repairing the hole with a patch and glue, then pumping the tire up with a hand pump.

Henry Ford, who is said to have despised dance music, nevertheless manufactured one of the favorite vehicles for small traveling bands—the Model T. Larger, more affluent bands traveled in big touring cars. Gene Goldkette used chartered buses to transport his big band. Bigger, more successful groups like Paul Whiteman's traveled by train.

The bands that spent a good deal of their time on the road playing engagements all over the country were known as "territory bands," and many big-name orchestras got their start this way. Jan Garber was one of the first bandleaders to take his band on one-night tours. Many territory bands were local units that covered a wide area in their own states but never made it into big time.

Coupled with the physical grind and hazards of road travel was economic insecurity. Most of the jobs in those early days were not controlled by the musicians' union and were played on commission with no guarantee. In other words, the band received part of the gate receipts, usually half. If the weather was good and a big crowd turned out, the band made money. Too often the crowd was disappointing or the dance was rained out. The band might drive five hundred miles to the next job, set up their instruments and find themselves playing for an empty house and no money. Your author can recall a long drive in a drafty bus to play for a dance that netted just enough to pay for one hamburger for each band member before starting the long trip home.

The musicians in the territory bands followed weather reports as anxiously as farmers. Rain and snow were the musicians' enemies. Many times the traveling band slipped and skidded in their Model T's over rain-soaked dirt roads, frequently having to take off their shoes, roll up their tuxedo trousers and wade the last half-mile to the dance hall carrying their instruments.

After playing for a dance, the long trip to the next engagement was an uncomfortable experience especially in cold weather. Trying to find a comfortable position, wedged among six other musicians in a small car with a cornet case poking the back of your neck and a music stand jabbing your ribs, took some maneuvering. Since cars in those days usually did not have heaters or defrosters, a trick for driving in subfreezing weather was to put a lighted candle on the dashboard on the theory that it would melt a small patch of ice from the windshield through which the driver could peer.

The country dance halls where many of the territory bands of the Midwest and Southwest played in the twenties, thirties and forties were not designed for the comfort of the musicians. They were square or octagonal barn-like structures with huge wooden shutters that could be raised in the summer to let the breeze in all around the sides. In winter they were closed; but through poor design, there was usually a gap around the edges through which the cold north wind would blow. The dancers who frequented these halls were hardy, rural people whose energetic dancing kept them warm; and if they needed additional heat, they could move to the far end of the hall where a big stove was situated—as far away from the bandstand as possible. The bandstand seemed always to be at the north end of the hall where the cracks in the walls were the widest. I can remember midwinter dances when it was so cold on the bandstand that we wore our overcoats and hats, and even the piano player kept on his gloves.

Bands on the road sometimes had a streak of bad luck, dances were rained out or flopped, and the musicians found themselves stranded with no way to pay the hotel bill and no money to get them to the next job. When this happened, the musicians' term was that they were "on panic." There are endless stories about bands on panic, trying to survive on a few cans of sardines while they figured a way to smuggle their instruments out past the watchful eye of the hotel clerk.

Endless mix-ups about booking engagements and minor and major catastrophes occurred. Instruments would fall off traveling buses. Jimmy McPartland tells about playing a dance during Prohibition where a trigger-happy gangster decided he wanted some target practice and shot the bass fiddle into kindling wood.

Leo Walker tells a story about Fred Waring's band, which traveled by train. They arrived in Buffalo to play; and shortly before they were to put on their uniforms, it was discovered that the baggage car with all their equipment had been taken off the train the night before at Harrisburg. The publicity man for Waring's band, Barney McDevitt, recalled that Rudy Vallee and his orchestra had played in Buffalo the night before and were still in the city. He rushed over and borrowed all of their instruments and uniforms so Waring's orchestra could go on. The only trouble was that Waring's tuba player was several payments behind on a tuba he had bought six months before in New York City. The music store had a branch in Buffalo and notified the store manager to repossess the instrument. Two men dashed over and tried to take the tuba away from Waring's man. "This isn't the tuba I bought from your store," the musician pleaded. "I borrowed it from Rudy Vallee." To which the finance men probably replied, "Hah!" and a backstage wrestling match over the tuba ensued. The hard-working publicity man managed to get an advance from Waring and save the tuba.

A story of unremitting catastrophe is told among musicians about a bandleader who booked a dance engagement at a hall some distance out in the country. Not having a regular band, he made a last-minute effort to round up some musicians. It happened to be a weekend when most musicians were working. The bandleader, himself a drummer, finally located a piano player and a saxophone player, both of whom were blind, and a trumpet player who was subject to epileptic seizures. By the time the harried leader had collected his musicians and loaded them and the instruments into his Model T, it was going to be nip and tuck to reach the dance hall on time. He drove as fast as the car would go, bouncing over the ruts in the dirt road. Suddenly, there was a blowout and the car screeched to a stop. The two blind musicians leaped out of the car in a panic and ran into a field where they got tangled in a barbed wire fence. The harrassed bandleader managed to rescue them, patch his blowout and arrive at the dance hall only an hour late. They were greeted by hostile glares from the farmers. The bandleader, by now a nervous wreck, finally got the instruments unpacked and the band ready. He heaved a sigh of relief, gave the downbeat for the band to start playing—whereupon the trumpet player fell down in an epileptic fit.

That story, like so many legends among musicians, may be somewhat exaggerated. But the hard life and dangers faced by jazz musicians making one-night stands is not fictitious. During the big-band era of the 1930's, bands traveled harder and further to make their one-nighters. Sometimes they drove five hundred miles with no time for sleep. Bandleader Hal Kemp was killed in a head-on collision on his way to his next engagement. Anson Weeks, driving hard to make a one-nighter in Iowa, was involved in a serious wreck that injured his arm so badly his career as a pianist-leader was virtually ended. The entire Jimmie Lunceford band was in a wreck that seriously injured several of its members. Red Nichols' band had a head-on crash with another car while making a one-night trip from Akron, Ohio, to Perth Amboy, N.J. The station wagon in which Isham Jones's orchestra traveled went out of control on a Georgia highway and was completely demolished, though luckily there were no serious injuries. Bessie Smith, was killed in an auto crash while traveling through Mississippi.

The hard traveling life of a jazz musician was summed up by Louis Armstrong for Richard Meryman of *Life* when he said:

> "And this life I got, few can do it, making those gigs sometime seven days a week—feel like I spent nine thousand hours on buses, planes, getting there just in time to play with cold chops, come off too tired to lift an eyelash—nothing but ringing and twisting and jumping and bumping . . . Every place you go . . ."

CHAPTER 14

BENNY GOODMAN AND THE KINGDOM OF SWING

It is 1936. America, floundering through the depression, has reelected Franklin D. Roosevelt to a second term as President, hoping that his New Deal will revive prosperity. There are long waiting lists at libraries for *Gone with the Wind,* the book that has topped the best-seller lists. Everyone is excited over the prospect that King Edward VIII of England might abdicate his throne to marry Mrs. Wallis Simpson—a king giving up his throne for the woman he loves! The big movies of the year are "The Great Ziegfeld," "The Story of Louis Pasteur" and "Anthony Adverse." Luise Rainer and Paul Muni are Academy Award winners. In Europe dark war clouds are gathering. There is civil war in Spain and Hitler has goose-stepped his German troops into the demilitarized Rhineland. But no one wants to think about the possibility of a second world war. They'd been more concerned with the outcome of the Olympics in Berlin and rooting for the Yankees who beat the Giants in the World Series. The song the nation is humming is a nonsensical little hit tune called "The Music Goes 'Round and 'Round."

But politics, movies, sports and books are forgotten by the teen-agers in America one night of each week—the night a program called "The Camel Caravan" unleashes on an eager radio audience the hot licks of "The King of Swing"—Benny Goodman. Edward VIII might be King of England, but Benny Goodman is the king of the "licorice stick" as far as the dance crowd is concerned. When the brilliant, fluid tones of his jazz clarinet cut through the swinging, big-band arrangement of his theme song "Let's Dance," the bobby-soxers go wild. Furniture is pushed aside and rugs rolled back to escape demolition by the jitterbuggers.

"Listen to that cat swing tonight."

"Yeah, he's really in the groove!"

"He's out of this world—he sends me!"

The era of big-band swing in America began on the night of August 21, 1935, at the Palomar Ballroom in Los Angeles when a surprised Benny Goodman found himself an overnight sensation. Beginning that night a completely new form of jazz swept the nation.

It is debatable how the term swing originated, but with it came a whole new vocabulary. If you "dug" this new "jive" and it sent you "out of this world," you were a "hep cat," but if not, you were "square." They danced the Lindy Hop, the shag, the Big Apple and the jitterbug; and the "bobby-soxers" went "peckin'" and "truckin' on down."

The Jazz Age was "out" and Swing was "in" and vast was the difference between the two. The hot jazz of the earlier Dixieland- and Chicago-style bands was the music of small groups playing unarranged, collective improvisations. Swing was the product of big bands and skillful arrangements.

From 1935 to 1945 was the decade of the big bands in America. Tommy and Jimmy Dorsey, Charlie Barnet, Harry James, Glenn Gray and the Casa Loma Orchestra, Bob Crosby, Les Brown, Count Basie, Artie Shaw, Woody Herman, Benny Goodman, Glenn Miller—these were the musical idols of the depression years and the Second World War. Out of the swing age came such vocalists as Frank Sinatra, Dick Haymes, Jo Stafford, Jimmy Rushing, Peggy Lee and Rosemary Clooney. The best known singing groups were the Andrews Sisters, the Four King Sisters, the Pied Pipers, the Mills Brothers and the Ink Spots.

Some of the hit songs that the public was singing and dancing to were "The Dipsy Doodle," "Christopher Columbus," "Music Maestro, Please," "Deep Purple," "Flat Foot Floogie," "And the Angels Sing," "Josephine" and the moving ballad of the war years "I'll Never Smile Again."

The big swing bands were full, smooth and solid and the music had organization and disciplined power. By comparison, the earlier, smaller jazz groups produced a disorganized effect: they were individuals going off on their own tangents in a lighter, more staccato fashion, giving the feeling that musical pandemonium had broken out within their ranks. Both styles relied on that all-important, basic jazz ingredient, the beat, although the big swing bands had gotten away from the two-beat rhythm entirely and used a rather heavy four beats to the measure. Benny Goodman believed the drummer was the most important man in the swing band and depended on the great drummer Gene Krupa as his cornerstone.

As always, changing music styles reflected changing times. The stock market crash ended the reckless, flamboyant mood of the Roaring Twenties. The repeal of prohibition in 1933 liberated jazz from the speakeasies and put it in the ballrooms and nightclubs. Although the nation was struggling through a grim depression and there was less money to spend, the people kept up their morale with music and dancing.

Will Rogers quipped that America was going to be the first nation in history to ride to the poorhouse in an automobile. He might have added that we were also going to insist that the poorhouse be equipped with radios and Saturday-night motion pictures, for those were the two new forms of entertainment that had captured America's imagination. Both brought music to a larger audience than ever before. Musicals were the most popular type of early talking pictures. One of the first was "The Jazz Singer," starring Al Jolson. Another early musical, already mentioned, was "The King of Jazz" featuring Paul Whiteman. A popular Tin Pan Alley song of the day was "If I Had a Talking Picture of You." The radio craze, gathering momentum since the twenties, had swept the nation from coast to coast by the early 1930's. When the listeners weren't laughing at Amos 'n' Andy, they were enjoying the melodious strains of Paul Whiteman, Guy Lombardo or the Cliquet Club Eskimos.

In both the talkies and the radio programs of the early 1930's, there was a preference for larger bands with a sweet sound. Ever since Paul Whiteman's outstanding success with his large, concert-style orchestra (the number of musicians in his orchestra eventually rose to thirty-four), popular bands had been getting larger. The bands that played a sweet, commercial style managed this without a great deal of difficulty. Their nine or ten men played arrangements that were simple, harmonized, gimmicked versions of the melody line. Their music was melodious, but it wasn't jazz. There was little improvisation and just enough rhythm for dancing but not enough to upset anyone.

Meanwhile, the hot jazzmen who took a dim view of these Mickey Mouse bands were having difficulty finding work. They either couldn't or wouldn't read music. Joseph "Wingy" Manone, the one-armed New Orleans trumpet player who could always be counted on for a pungent observation, once said indignantly, "I can read the notes; I just can't separate 'em—five flats look like a bunch of grapes to me."

This cavalier attitude toward the written note was fine so long as the band was small and everyone was improvising. It works with a small group of, say, five or six men. But it becomes impracticable if the band grows much larger. A band of twelve musicians all improvising in different directions becomes too complicated to follow. The small band soloists did not necessarily have to read music; but the big bands demanded technical reading skill of the sidemen. These bands introduced a new figure to the jazz scene—the arranger.

An "arrangement" is a predetermined manner and order in which jazz musicians decide to perform a tune. This might include variations on the melody as well as interesting introductions and endings. A few Dixieland groups such as Red Nichols' and Bob Crosby's Bobcats used "head arrangements" worked out in a flexible style at rehearsals and memorized. But as the bands grew larger and more complex, it became necessary to write out the arrangements.

The person who did this was highly talented and an important figure because his style would determine how well the band would swing. The arranger was a combination composer and stylist. He had to have a thorough knowledge of harmony and composition. The "voicing" he wrote—that is the harmonic relationship of the instruments in the band—gave the group its distinctive sound. For example, the unique sound of the Glenn Miller band depended upon a special voicing of the reed section—a clarinet in the upper register playing in harmonic relationship with the saxophones. The best swing arrangers were expert at blending the ensemble with the jazz soloists. Duke Ellington is a master at this. Among other great arrangers were Fletcher Henderson, Sy Oliver, Benny Carter, Jimmy Munday, Buck Clayton, Don Redman and Billy Strayhorn.

Some of the earlier jazzmen who were used to playing by ear, or faking, had trouble reading the arrangements. However, one who had not the slightest difficulty in reading notes was clarinetist Benny Goodman, a child prodigy who made his first professional appearance at twelve. He studied the clarinet seriously and is one of those rare musicians who is as fine a classical musician as he is a jazz soloist. Goodman is equally at home on a concert stage and in a smoke-filled nightclub jamming a scorching version of "China Boy."

Benny left Chicago in the late twenties, worked around New York with various jazz groups, and then began to assemble his own orchestra. He liked the idea of a big band—the problem was how to make a big band play jazz? Fortunately, there were large bands that had learned how to swing together in Harlem even in the 1920's. Outstanding among their bandleaders were Fletcher Henderson and Duke Ellington. Goodman was greatly influenced by Henderson and his arranger Don Redman. In fact, Benny owed much of his success to arrangements he bought from Fletcher Henderson. Goodman was a perfectionist and rehearsed his band on these arrangements until the band achieved a noteworthy synchronization and polish.

The big bands used an average of four saxophones and five brass instruments, usually three trumpets and two trombones. The arrangements were often written in four-part harmony. This gave the band powerful voices to work with, but the problem was producing authentic jazz sounds with such a large group. Henderson and Redman worked out patterns of big-band teamwork that went back to the basic jazz traditions. One was the call-and-response pattern. The saxophone section would play a rhythmic phrase and the brass would reply and the two sections would go on answering one another in fine, swinging style that built to a powerful climax.

The phrases tossed back and forth between the reed and brass sections were called riffs and the art of riffing became one of the principal jazz devices of the big swing bands. A "riff" is a musical phrase generally of four-bar duration and dates straight back to the blues tradition. Some examples of classic big-band swing tunes built on riffs are the "One O'Clock Jump," "In the Mood" and "Woodchoppers' Ball." If you listen carefully to these numbers you will notice the melody is a simple rhythmic phrase of a few notes repeated over and over. Just as Beethoven built the magnificent opening theme of his Fifth Symphony on three notes repeated in different ways, so Fletcher Henderson built his swinging arrangements on the riff—a method that was carried to artistic heights by Duke Ellington and Count Basie.

However, improvisation still remained the high point of swing experience. When the jazzman stood up to take his solo, the band played a background pattern of rhythmic riffs. Instead of having only the rhythm section behind him as in the smaller jazz groups, he was now backed up by the whole big band.

By 1934 Benny Goodman had put together a swinging big band that was really in the groove. The public, however, reacted with monumental indifference. Swing had not yet caught on. Who had ever heard of Benny Goodman? He played an engagement for less than scale wages at Billy Rose's Music Hall; and he got a booking at the Hotel Roosevelt in New York City where the waiters complained he played too loud.

Meanwhile, his band had signed for a weekly radio job on the "Let's Dance" program sponsored by the National Biscuit Company. The program was on the air every Saturday night from eleven until two in the morning, carried by fifty-three stations from coast to coast. Three bands were featured: the first two played Latin rhythms and sweet dance music; and in the last part of the program, Benny Goodman came on with his big swing band. The program turned out to be much more of a break than the band realized at the time.

But in the early summer of 1935, success did not appear to be included in Benny's destiny. He was booked on a series of one-night stands all the way to the West Coast. The tour was a disaster. His music was met with either indifference or outright hostility. Weary and disheartened, morale at a low ebb, the band arrived for the final date in the tour at the Palomar Ballroom in Los Angeles. When they took their first look at the ballroom, their gloom turned to panic. The dance floor looked large enough to land an airplane. For the first hour, the band timidly played soft, sweet tunes, hoping they wouldn't get tossed out. The crowd ignored them.

Suddenly, Benny decided he'd had it up to here. The tour had been one grand flop from beginning to end. This might well be the last night he'd be able to hold the band together. If so, they were going out in style, having a good time, playing the kind of music they liked. He called out the big, Fletcher Henderson arrangements. Facing the band, he gave the downbeat and the band exploded with the full, driving force of their kind of jazz. The whole band caught the mood—they'd never played better.

Then Goodman became aware of a commotion on the dance floor. He turned and to his astonishment saw a tide of yelling, cheering young dancers crowding around the bandstand. This was the kind of Benny Goodman music they had been waiting for! Some began doing the West Coast version of the Lindy. Others watched and listened to the band. Goodman later wrote, "The first big roar from the crowd was one of the sweetest sounds I ever heard in my life . . ."

The band was amazed to discover that they were already well known on the West Coast and the crowd had been anticipating their swing arrangements. This was the result of the "Let's Dance" program and a matter of time zones that the band had overlooked. Their broadcast in New York started too late to attract many listeners in the East. But because of the time difference, the program was heard on the West Coast from eight until eleven on Saturday nights, just when kids turned on their radios for dance music. These live broadcasts, plus records of the Goodman band played by disc jockeys, had made them popular with the West Coast crowd and laid the groundwork for their personal appearance.

Following this success, the fame of Benny Goodman and swing swept the country. Soon one could turn on the radio almost any night and hear the live music of big bands performing in night spots across the nation. Most of the bandleaders were, themselves, outstanding jazz soloists. A slender young man named Artie Shaw became Benny Goodman's chief rival on clarinet and vied for the King-of-Swing crown. Shaw came on the air with a haunting theme "Nightmare," and made a smash hit record of "Begin the Beguine." He got as much front-page publicity from his many marriages as he did from his music. Among his wives were Hollywood actresses Lana Turner, Ava Gardner and Evelyn Keyes and authoress Kathleen Winsor. Another clarinet-playing bandleader Woody Herman made the scene with his popular "Woodchoppers' Ball." Everyone recognized Tommy Dorsey's smooth, high-register trombone playing his theme "I'm Gettin' Sentimental

Over You." A young singer on the Dorsey band named Frank Sinatra, who sported a bow tie and looked as if he weighed all of ninety pounds dripping wet, was responsible for mass swooning of bobby-soxers wherever he appeared. Jimmy Dorsey, Tommy's brother, a superb jazz clarinetist and saxophonist, led his own successful big band. He became identified with the popular hit tune "So Rare."

Despite the overwhelming popularity of the big, powerful bands, there remained a lingering nostalgia for the small, contrapuntal jazz groups. Many of the large bands satisfied this need by featuring a band within the band. Tommy Dorsey had his Clambake Seven, which played a near-Dixieland style. Bing Crosby's kid brother Bob came the closest to keeping Dixieland alive during those swing years with his excellent group The Bobcats, which, incidentally, is still around and going strong. Artie Shaw, always one for musical experimentation, had his Gramercy Five, which included, of all things, a harpsichord.

Another musical rage of the 1930's was "boogie-woogie," a piano style which used a rolling, eight-beats-to-the-measure left-hand rhythm. It was by no means new. The style grew from early church music, blues singers and honky-tonk piano players. But the general public was not familiar with it. Jazz writer and critic John Hammond first heard it on a record called "Honky Tonk Train Blues," and began a search for Meade Lux Lewis, who composed and recorded the tune. After some time Hammond found him washing cars in a Chicago garage. Hammond urged Lewis to make a new recording of "Honky Tonk Train" which started boogie-woogie on its way to popularity.

Meade Lux Lewis, Pete Johnson and Albert Ammons were the top exponents of boogie-woogie; and during the 1930's all achieved considerable fame. However, the author of one of the best-known boogie-woogie tunes "Pinetop's Boogie-Woogie" was not around to enjoy the popular acclaim. He was Clarence "Pinetop" Smith, a pioneer of the rhythmic eight-beats-to-the-bar style. His are some of the best boogie-woogie records made during the late 1920's. Smith was playing in Chicago in 1929 when a brawl broke out and he was killed by a stray bullet while seated at the piano.

The big bands soon had boogie-woogie arrangements and produced such hits as "Bumble Boogie," "Beat Me Daddy Eight to the Bar" and the "Yancey Special."

The big-band sound was the folk music of the American armed forces during World War II. Soldiers danced to swing records on juke boxes in USO halls; Glenn Miller's recordings of "In the Mood," "Tuxedo Junction" and "String of Pearls" brought them a little closer to home. Ironically, Glenn Miller died while bringing his music still closer to the soldiers overseas. In 1944, he took off on a flight from England to France and disappeared forever, presumably shot down.

During the decade of the big bands, Benny Goodman remained the king of swing. He was at the height of his popularity from 1936 to 1944. One success followed another: a triumphant return to New York following his wild reception in California, a jazz concert at Carnegie Hall, a weekly radio show called "The Camel Caravan," huge record sales and a Hollywood movie based on his life and music.

Goodman featured many great jazz soloists, among them trumpet players Bunny Berigan, Harry James and Ziggy Elman, drummer Gene Krupa and pianists Jess Stacy, Mell Powell and Johnny Guarnieri. Many of these graduated from Goodman's band to become leaders of their own groups.

Goodman was the first big-band leader to break the bias against integrated bands, even though he encountered some public opposition. He hired many excellent

Negro jazz musicians: pianist Teddy Wilson, trumpet player Cootie Williams and vibraphonist Lionel Hampton. Even the famous Count Basie joined Goodman to play piano at some memorable recording sessions. It was a touch of irony that Count Basie wrote and recorded "One O'Clock Jump" with only moderate success; and a few months later, Goodman recorded the same tune and it became his first record to sell over a million copies.

While "Mr. B. G." made his greatest contribution to the swing movement with his big band, he also played some fine jazz in small groups within the big band. There was the trio which included Krupa on drums, Teddy Wilson on piano and Goodman on clarinet; the quartet added Hampton's exciting jazz vibraphone; and the sextet added guitarist Charlie Christian and trumpeter Williams.

Benny Goodman remains one of the great jazz clarinetists of all time. His astounding technical ability and his originality of style greatly influenced other clarinet jazzmen during the thirties and forties. The highest compliment a jazz clarinetist could receive was to be told he sounded like Benny Goodman. His name will remain forever synonymous with swing.

CHAPTER 15

THE ROYALTY OF JAZZ

The kingdom of jazz has its royal family. Bessie Smith was its empress and there have been a number of kings. But there is only one count, one duke and one earl. Of all the big bands, the ones led by Count Basie and Duke Ellington have been the most durable and have played the most profound jazz. And all the jazz pianists around today are indebted to the keyboard genius of Earl "Fatha" Hines, who is indeed the father of the modern jazz piano.

Styles in jazz come and go. Jazz experts argue over the relative merits of Dixieland, bop, swing and cool jazz. Meanwhile Count Basie and Duke Ellington, each in his own distinctive style, go on playing music that is continually fresh, exciting and meaningful. William "Count" Basie was born in Red Bank, New Jersey, in 1904, and was given his first piano lessons by his mother. He began his professional career in the early 1920's playing at Harlem night spots, sometimes accompanying Bessie Smith. It was during this period that he came under the influence of the fabulous pianist Fats Waller, who taught him many things, including Waller's trademark the powerful, stride bass.

Fats Waller had one of the most powerful left hands in the music business. Eddie Condon tells about giving a party in New York. The front was removed from a rented piano to give more volume. During the course of the evening, Fats dropped by and livened things up by playing and singing some of his inimitable jazz. The next morning when Condon cleaned up the wreckage of the party, he discovered piano hammers all over the room. They had broken under the impact of Waller's sledgehammer left!

Stride bass dates back to ragtime piano, but modern pianists use it effectively when playing strong rhythm. James P. Johnson, a piano giant of Waller's day and Waller's mentor, was a master of ragtime-based stride. He and Fats played very much alike and both are rated high in the annals of jazz.

But in the mid-1920's, a new voice came from the piano. It was to influence Count Basie and every jazz pianist to the present day. It was the utterly original style of Earl Hines giving the piano the same range of jazz expression that Satchmo gave the trumpet and Teagarden the trombone. Before Earl only two pianists made much of a lasting contribution to jazz. One was Jelly Roll Morton who expanded ragtime styles to reproduce the traditional jazz sounds of the New Orleans brass marching bands on the keyboard. The other, already mentioned, was James P. Johnson who in turn taught Waller.

Before this, the jazz piano was chiefly a solo instrument heard in bars, honky-tonks and silent-movie houses. When included in a band, it was used for rhythm accompaniment, similar to the banjo. Earl Hines brought a whole new concept of jazz possibilities for the piano. Departing radically from ragtime tradition, Hines gave the piano a solo voice that reflected the trumpet phrasing of Armstrong. He played the piano like a horn, expressing beautiful jazz ideas and hot licks; and the instrument took a much more important role in the jazz ensemble.

Hines was born in Duquesne, Pennsylvania, in 1905. When he was nine he started taking piano lessons. He advanced so rapidly that his teacher soon had him working on the difficult Czerny books of piano exercises. This rigorous training was the foundation for Hines's later facility on the keyboard. He was still a teen-ager when he began his professional career. In 1926 he was in Chicago, playing in the Carroll Dickerson band that had Darnell Howard on clarinet and alto sax, Honoré Dutrey on trombone, Tubby Hall on drums and Louis Armstrong on trumpet. Armstrong took over leadership of the band in 1927 and made Hines musical director. This group became the top Negro jazz combo in Chicago. The young, white musicians who were developing Chicago-style jazz came to worship and learn from them. Meanwhile, Hines was recording with Louis Armstrong and his fame was spreading rapidly to all corners of the jazz world. His style soon became so highly regarded that unless a pianist played like Hines he was apt to have trouble finding work. So many pianists were copying Hines's style that he began to sound as if he were copying himself!

Earl Hines has continued to delight jazz fans right up to the present. In 1966 a longtime fan of Hines's, Leonard V. Martin offered him a most unusual, lifetime contract. It guarantees Hines twenty thousand dollars a year for the rest of his life for playing ten months each year at The Cannery, a shopping and dining center near Fisherman's Wharf in San Francisco, and leaves him free to arrange outside tours the other two months. This contract is a testimony to the esteem jazz lovers have for Fatha Hines.

In the late 1920's, with the piano tradition of Johnson, Waller and Hines to inspire him, Count Basie left New York for Kansas City. Here his career really got under way with the great bands of that region, especially the Bennie Moten band.

From 1927 to 1938, Kansas City was a wide-open town, kept that way by gangsters and a political machine. It was also a hotbed of jazz. The depression didn't affect the Kansas City mobsters and they could afford to pay good wages to the musicians who played in their nightclubs. Kansas City was a focal point of a dance territory that took in Texas, Oklahoma, Arkansas and Missouri. The dancers in this region liked their music strong and hot. So big bands in this area were playing their version of swing a number of years before Benny Goodman became popular, and they were able to survive the depression while jazz musicians in the East were going hungry or fleeing to Europe.

In this rich jazz climate, Count Basie cut his musical teeth. When Bennie Moten died in 1935, the Count formed his own large band and headed back to New York. He was an immediate success; and except for a few shaky periods, Basie's band has continued to be one of the top big bands in the nation.

By the late 1930's Count Basie had developed his characteristic playing style: a few sharp, bright notes or chords with his right hand to punctuate choruses given over to the rhythm section. The whole band seems to pause and hold its breath and one hears a brief tinkle from the Count's right hand. This spare, restrained piano coupled with one of the best rhythm sections in the business (drums, bass and guitar) has given the Basie band a solidity and purposeful drive all its own. His saxophone and brass sections have carried the art of riffing to its ultimate perfection.

The Count has always featured soloists of the highest calibre. Tenor-sax stars in his band have included Lester

Young, Don Byas, Buddy Tate, Illinois Jacquet and Paul Gonsalves. In the trumpet section, such jazzmen as Al Killian, Joe Newman, Emmett Berry, Thad Jones and Joe Wilder have appeared. On trombones, Basie has featured Vic Dickenson, J. J. Johnson, Benny Powell and Henry Coker.

In the kingdom of jazz, Duke Ellington occupies the loftiest spot. He has been a successful jazz pianist and bandleader since the 1920's; but much more than that, he is a composer and arranger of unique distinction. Ellington is one of the true geniuses of jazz music. As a composer and arranger he has undoubtedly made the greatest contribution to jazz of anyone who has lived. His music has a rare, haunting quality. "Mood Indigo" (his first popular hit back in 1930), "Solitude," "Sophisticated Lady" and "In a Sentimental Mood" are but a few of the many Ellington compositions that have scored a lasting popular appeal. Over the years, he has composed more than a thousand tunes.

Edward Kennedy Ellington is his full name, but when he was a youngster, a neighborhood friend called him Duke, and it would be difficult to find a more fitting and descriptive nickname. Born in Washington, D.C., in 1899, his family was fairly well-to-do and could afford schooling for Edward. At first he considered a career as a commercial illustrator, but also studied music. In his late teens he was earning money both by painting signs and playing dance engagements. Gradually music absorbed more of his interest. In the spring of 1923, Fats Waller persuaded Duke to move to Manhattan and devote himself entirely to music, and he has been a successful bandleader ever since. It was during its long (1927–32) engagement at the Cotton Club on Lenox Avenue in Harlem that the Ellington band became nationally known. They broadcast directly from the club and recorded regularly.

What makes Ellington unique is his ability to express

musical ideas through his band as if it were an extension of himself. All his arrangements are tailored to the style and temperament of his musicians. With a change in personnel, he might completely rewrite some arrangements to fit the new musician better.

No other composer-arranger uses Ellington's approach. The Duke knows that jazz musicians are individualists. For example, ten, formally trained, symphonic oboe players will produce tones as alike as peas in a pod. But ten jazz musicians will be ten individualists both in style of improvisation and instrument tone. One might play with a rich, gutty timbre, another with a smoother, more liquid tone, a third with a thin, cool sound and so on. Rather than discourage the individualism of his men, the Duke arranges for their tonal quality. He "voices" his orchestrations in such a manner that the individual tone of each man is essential to the overall effect. As a result, the Ellington orchestra has a tonal quality that has never been duplicated. An Ellington arrangement played by any other group, no matter how professional, would not have the same lavish sound as when done by Ellington's own group.

This does not entirely explain the Ellington phenomena, of course, because the man's genius as a composer and his deep understanding of harmonic effects is equally important.

Ellington's orchestra has always exhibited a splendid array of outstanding soloists, among them Harry Carney, who has played baritone saxophone in Ellington's band since 1926! Other jazzmen who have performed with the group include Ben Webster (tenor sax), Ray Nance (trumpet and jazz violin), Barney Bigard (clarinet and saxophone), Cootie Williams (trumpet), Charlie Shavers (trumpet) and Louis Bellson (drums). The top-rated musicians who passed through the Ellington ranks would by themselves fill a jazz hall of fame.

It would be difficult to single out any of Ellington's men for special mention, but one can hardly go through the list without an added word about Johnny "Rabbit" Hodges whom critics list with Benny Carter as top alto-saxophonists. The alto saxophone is one of the most difficult instruments on which to play good jazz. Smaller and lighter than the tenor sax, it sounds insipid and whiny in the hands of most musicians. It lacks character. But when played by Hodges it becomes a powerful jazz voice. His tone is incredibly rich and full. His flow of exquisite, melodic ideas just about equals Armstrong's, and his blues are the real thing. When he wants to, he can play with a drive that is fantastic. One of the best demonstrations of this drive is his recording of "All of Me" made with a small ensemble of his own. Many of Ellington's arrangements are written around Hodges and feature him throughout. One thinks of Johnny Hodges in relation to the alto saxophone as Armstrong to the trumpet, Hines to the piano, Jack Teagarden to the trombone and Coleman Hawkins to the tenor saxophone.

In 1939, Duke Ellington began a long period of fruitful collaboration with arranger Billy Strayhorn. To the general public, Strayhorn is perhaps best known for his composition "Take the 'A' Train" which became the theme song for the Ellington orchestra. Behind the scenes, however, Strayhorn was a major source of ideas and arrangements. The two men thought so much alike musically it was almost unbelievable. Duke Ellington described this rapport, to AP writer Mary Campbell:

> "It got to the point where the critics would say, 'Duke shouldn't have done that on the piano, on a record, and it would have been Billy [they were talking about]. He didn't play any jobs, just records. Or they'd say, 'Billy wrote such and such,' and I would

> have written it. We said, 'Let's don't tell them any more who did which.' Now I want to do a record of Strayhorn originals and some of them I can't figure out if they're his compositions or mine."

It was a sad personal and professional blow to Ellington when Billy Strayhorn died of cancer in May of 1967.

But Ellington doesn't let life get him down. An urbane and cultured man, he is as irrepressible and enthusiastic as ever. He enjoys working under pressure. He told Miss Campbell:

> "I always have to have deadlines. I wrote 'Black and Tan Fantasy' in a taxi coming down through Central Park on my way to the recording studio. I'd been in an after-hours joint all night and I had to write it. That was in 1928 when staying up twenty-four hours a day didn't mean anything."

Although Ellington is now in his late sixties, he still often works twelve to fifteen hours a day with as much relish and enthusiasm as when he started.

The Ellington band travels a great deal: to Africa in 1966 to represent the United States at the World Festival of Negro Arts in Dakar, Senegal, to America's West Coast to play location jobs in the fall of 1967. The band plays jazz, it swings, it plays the blues, and it appears in the country's leading concert halls and recently even in churches!

For a number of years, beginning in 1943, Ellington's band gave annual concerts at Carnegie Hall in New York. His first major composition for this type of appearance was "Black, Brown, and Beige," an extended jazz composition lasting about fifty minutes in its original form. It transformed the elements of jazz into a work suitable for the concert hall.

Another work of this nature is "Suite Thursday" composed by Ellington and Strayhorn when the directors of the Monterey Jazz Festival commissioned an original Ellington work to be presented in 1960. Monterey, California, is closely associated with author John Steinbeck who wrote many of his early books while living in that area; and it was Steinbeck's novel *Sweet Thursday* which inspired the title for Ellington's jazz suite.

The suite is in four parts. The first, called "Misfit Blues," features Lawrence Brown's trombone and a piano solo. The reed section predominates during much of this part with some interesting trumpet work by Willie Cook, all in a rocking tempo. The Duke says it describes Steinbeck as a swinger. The first section ends with a smashing brass chord. Part Two, called "Schwiphti" [Swifty], has a fast, flying pace sparked with Ellington piano passages, solos by Paul Gonsalves on tenor sax and Ray Nance on trumpet. This section, Duke contends, proves that Cannery Row had a tempo. The third part of the suite is called "Zweet Zurzday" and begins with a Latin beat. The tempo changes to 4/4 time for a reed chorus and trombone, clarinet and tenor sax solos. Duke's program notes say this part describes episodes from the Steinbeck novel: the clarinet solo is "the beautiful dream" or "the fuzz of imagination" and the tenor-sax solo is "the fog that clouds it." The final part, entitled "Lay-by," features a thrilling Ray Nance violin solo all the way. It is a marvelous example of the Nance's genius on an instrument that rarely sounds good playing jazz.

A more recent Ellington concert-jazz work was composed with Strayhorn in 1963 after a fifteen-week State Department tour. It is entitled "The Far East Suite." In

1965, Ellington conducted the New York Philharmonic in the premiere of a new composition "The Golden Broom and the Green Apple," a humorous tale about a city chick and a country girl.

Two Episcopal priests, after hearing Ellington's band in a nightclub in California, asked him to write a jazz musical service for Grace Cathedral in San Francisco. His composition "In the Beginning God," based on the thunderous opening words of Genesis, was first performed in 1965 and has been in great demand both in this country and in Europe ever since. Its success has inspired the Duke to work on more jazz works suitable for church performance.

It is an interesting sidelight that jazz, which had its roots in Negro churches and made the rounds of Storyville's honky-tonks, Chicago's speakeasies and Kansas City's gangster-run nightclubs, has completed the circle back to the churches where it began.

CHAPTER 16

THE BLUES

The blues is a song late at night in a lonely river-bottom shack. The blues is a state of mind. The blues is a a way of singing about life. When a man lands in a chain gang, he sings the blues. When his best girl leaves him, or his friend double-crosses him, or his money runs out, or the river floods, or he's got a new job in another city and he's homesick, he puts his troubles into a certain kind of folk song that has a special haunting quality all its own.

When jazz came along, the blues were already here. The blues became a part of jazz, so deeply imbedded they flavored all its forms from the earliest Dixieland.

Nobody can say for sure when the blues began. They may have started with slaves in the fields, who had a way of singing a long, high call that cracked or broke on a falsetto note, producing such a lonely, lost sound it would give the listener a chill down his spine. That shout, called the field cry or holler, may well have carried over into the blues song.

Gospel singing was a part of it, too, a very important part of jazz and the blues. Listen to Mahalia Jackson, the magnificent lady who has dedicated her life to songs of praise to the Lord. When she appears in her long, white gown and raises her rich voice in gospel singing—the Negro spirituals of her people—there is the power and drive of the jazz beat, the distant echo of the field cry and the unmistakable poignant, haunting quality of the blues. Her voice wavers and dips over the heartbreaking cry of the blue notes. Her singing is living testimony that the blues—and jazz—came every bit as much from churches as from honky-tonks.

When the slaves combined spirituals and field cries with the European ballad form, a very earthy kind of improvisational folk singing gradually evolved. It gave the singer a personal way to tell about his life and the things that troubled him and gave him the blues. But he could put irony and laughter into it too, to prove that life couldn't get a man down if he kept his sense of humor and sang in the right way.

The blues, to begin with, was the music of southern, country people who took their songs with them when they wandered to the cities after the Civil War. Most of the early blues singers long ago slipped into anonymity. They were ex-slaves, drifters, singing on street corners, in dance halls and in Negro theaters—sometimes earning a little money at it. They had forsaken the banjo for the guitar, an instrument better suited to the blues. Where the banjo has a straightforward, ringing, plunking sound, the guitar strings could be made to waver and twang in a blues-y manner. Some of the blues singers pressed knife blades or bottle necks against the strings to make them wail.

In those days, a Negro had to have a strong back to work at the few jobs open to him. If he were handicapped, there was not much he could do except beg on street corners. Playing a guitar helped attract attention. Some street beggers added a real talent for singing the blues to their playing. For example, there was Blind Lemon Jefferson, one of the first primitive blues singers to gain some national fame. He was born in Galveston, Texas, in 1885, and he wandered around singing wherever people would listen. He was poor most of his life. In the 1930's, Blind Lemon made some records that sold well in Negro neighborhoods, and he had a brief period of prosperity before drifting off and dying in obscurity. He was the first of the primitive country blues singers to record. On records he left an earthy style that showed what the blues sounded like before jazz was born. Some of the songs he recorded were "Hangman's Blues," "Rabbit Foot Blues," "Southern Woman Blues," "Black Snake Moon" and the "Long, Lonesome Blues."

One of Blind Lemon Jefferson's disciples was Huddie Ledbetter, known as Leadbelly, who became quite famous among the early country blues singers. Born in Mooringsport, Louisiana, around 1888, Leadbelly had an adventurous life, a good deal of it spent in southern jails. His family moved to Texas when Leadbelly was five, and his first adventure was to run away from home at an early age. Around 1905 he met Blind Lemon Jefferson who taught him how to play guitar and sing the blues. For a while, Leadbelly acted as Blind Lemon's eyes as the two traveled and performed together.

But Leadbelly couldn't stay out of trouble. From 1918 to 1925, he served a prison sentence for murder and then was pardoned. He worked in some Gulf Coast cities for a while but his violent streak got him in trouble again and he was back in jail. Legend has it that, in 1934, the Governor of Louisiana heard Leadbelly play and sing and was so impressed by his talent that he granted a pardon; but most historians say Leadbelly received a routine discharge. In any case, Leadbelly wandered East and got a job as chauffeur for John A. Lomax, a collector and archivist of folk music. Leadbelly became a protégé of Lomax, who arranged for him to record for the Library of Congress. During the 1940's, Leadbelly sang in nightclubs and even made a successful concert tour of France before his death in New York in 1949.

There were other primitive country blues singers and guitar pickers: Barbecue Bob, Blind Willie McTell, Peg Leg Howell, Blind Boy Fuller, Bukka White and others, some from Louisiana, some from Mississippi, others from Georgia, Alabama and Texas. When the phonograph industry became big business in the 1920's, it discovered a profitable market among the Negro population for blues records. Recording companies latched onto all the blues singers they could find in the large northern cities. Some companies even packed their equipment on trucks and went combing backcountry roads in the rural South, looking for blues singers. The discs they made were called "race records" because they were made especially for the Negro population, and they spread the fame of many blues singers who might otherwise have been known only in their own neighborhoods.

Race records immortalized the songs of the most famous woman blues singer in jazz history, the incomparable Bessie Smith. Bessie was a lady with a big body, a big voice and a big heart, who lived the blues she sang. She was born of a very poor family in Chattanooga, Tennessee, on April 15, 1894. She learned how to sing the blues from Ma Rainey. In the 1920's, Bessie Smith enjoyed periods of great prosperity, earning as much as two thousand dollars a week. When she made a record, lines a block long would form in Negro neighborhoods outside the stores that sold her recordings. She was accompanied on these records by some of the greatest jazz musicians—Louis Armstrong, clarinetist Buster Bailey, pianist James P. Johnson and the Fletcher Henderson band. She had a deep, poignant voice and sang with tremendous feeling and power. But she drank too much and threw her money away like a child in a candy store. She was generous to a fault.

In the 1930's, Bessie's career fell on hard times. The fickle public became interested in radio and the movies and lost interest in the blues. She could find engagements only in second-rate nightclubs. Finally, in 1937, while on a tour through Mississippi, she was involved in an automobile accident and bled to death before she could be given medical attention. But when Bessie Smith was at the peak of her career, she was known as "the Empress of the Blues." Louis Armstrong said she could stand in front of a microphone all day and make up blues songs and give them titles and they would all be hits. She made a total of 159 record sides, all masterpieces of blues singing.

While nobody knows for certain when this style of folk singing began to be called the blues, the first time it appeared on sheet music was when W. C. Handy, "the Father of the Blues," published a song called "Memphis Blues" in 1912.

Handy was not a blues singer. He was a cornet player who played in brass bands and minstrel bands and later led dance orchestras. He was born in Alabama in 1873. When he first declared his wish to become a musician, his strongly religious father shouted that he'd rather see him dead! But Handy learned the cornet anyway, studying at the Kentucky Music College, as well as reading all the instruction books he could lay his hands on.

In 1896, when he was twenty-three years old, Handy joined Mahara's Minstrel Troupe. In his travels with this troupe, he heard many primitive blues singers. The blues made a strong impression on him. He began to collect traditional blues songs and to compose his own. Where blues singers like Blind Lemon Jefferson and Leadbelly carried their repertoire in their heads, Handy had the wisdom and ability to write down his compositions and publish them. Sheet music versions of Handy's blues songs became widely popular and circulated the blues to a white audience. This gave Handy a more permanent reputation than the wandering blues singers ever attained. The royalties from his blues songs made him quite comfortable financially in his later years. He died in 1958, and his funeral was attended by many celebraties from the entertainment world.

By 1914, the year Handy wrote what became the best-known blues song in the world "St. Louis Blues," the singing and playing of the blues had settled into a standard form among musicians. The chorus was twelve measures long; and the accompaniment, or "blues changes," consisted of the three most basic chords in European music—the tonic, sub-dominant and dominant chords. When a jazzman sees that a tune has blues changes he knows what notes he can play when he improvises. He knows the pattern will be twelve measures in length and how the chords will resolve one to another.

However, not all tunes, which have the word blues in the title can be played to the accompaniment of the standard blues changes. "Sugar Blues," for example, is not a true blues tune either in mood or chord progressions; it falls more into the category of a novelty tune. Most boogie-woogie piano players stick to standard blues progressions in their compositions; but on the other hand, some of the early, wandering, primitive blues singers used various other chord progressions to accompany their songs.

But in the most familiar blues style, the words of the song follow a pattern fitted into the twelve-bar limitation. These twelve bars are broken into three sections of four measures each. In the first four measures, the singer makes a statement:

"My gal's got me down; I'm singin' the blues all day."

In the next four-measure phrase the statement is usually repeated exactly:

"My gal's got me down; I'm singin' the blues all day."

Some musicians think this practice dates back to the early days when the blues singer made up the words as he went along. By repeating the first statement, he gave himself time to think of an ending for his little story; at the same time, it built up a certain tension in the listener as he waited to see how the song would end. Then would follow the final four bar section which completes the song:

"I'm goin' to the river, to wash my troubles away."

There is something else that sets the blues apart from other folk songs and gives it that distinctive, haunting quality. This is a sound often referred to as the blue note. The blue note crept into jazz from the very beginning and was responsible for the low-down quality. "Blue notes" are usually flatted third and seventh notes of the major scale; but the fifth note can also be flatted.

These notes receive special treatment by the blues singer—his voice dips over them, flatting them by a quarter- to a half-tone, resulting in the distinctive sound of a minor key played against the background of a major key accompaniment. This produces a pleasantly dissonant sound, characteristic of jazz music. Perhaps in these blue notes, we hear the echo of the field cry of bygone days.

Some experts believe that the slaves, who were used to the pentatonic scale of African music, had difficulty adjusting to the diatonic European scale with its half-tones. The third and seventh tones gave the Afro-American singers trouble, and they tended to flatten them. Whether there is truth to this theory or not, jazz would not have the sound it does without blue notes and the tradition of the blues.

When a jazzman plays a blues solo, he makes use of the flatted third and seventh notes of the scale just as singers do when their voices dip over these notes. The real test of a jazz musician is how well he can play the blues. He may have considerable technical ability and be a polished musician as far as reading notes are concerned. He may even be able to improvise, but it's the blues that separate the men from the boys. Unless he can play the blues with this true sound and feeling, there is something lacking in him as a jazz soloist.

Of all the instrumentalists associated with the blues, one stands out above the rest—the great trombonist Jack Teagarden. He was one of the few white men to get the soul of Negro blues in his playing.

Born in Vernon, Texas, in 1905, Jack was a big, slow-moving guy who never lost his Texas drawl. He began fooling around with the trombone at the age of seven and was largely self-taught. His family said Jack learned the blues by sitting on a fence behind a Negro holy-roller congregation night after night and listening to the gospel singing and shouting.

He worked in his father's cotton gin for a while, then as a garage mechanic in Oklahoma City and as a motion picture projectionist in San Angelo, Texas. Mechanics and electronics fascinated him all his life, but music was his real love. By the time he was sixteen, he was playing professionally. He had a job at the Horn Palace in San Antonio until an old-fashioned Western shoot-out convinced him that it wasn't a very healthy spot.

He moved on to Houston where he played with Peck Kelley's Bad Boys. The bandleader, pianist Peck Kelley, is one of the mystery figures of jazz history. Musicians and critics who heard him play insist he was one of the greatest jazz pianists who lived, but Kelley turned down offer after offer to leave Houston, and like Freddie Keppard, refused to make records, so we have no permanent evidence of his ability. It was while playing with Kelley's band in 1921 that Jack Teagarden began to team up with top jazzmen, such as Pee Wee Russell.

From Houston, Jack drifted to Chicago where he astounded the leading jazz musicians with his fantastic technique and original style. According to musical legend, when Jack first arrived in Chicago, Pee Wee Russell took him around to a bar where musicians hung out. Jack came in wearing a terrible-looking cap and overcoat that he'd brought from Texas. His trombone case was under his arm. Somebody asked him if he knew how to play the instrument he was carrying. In his lazy, good-natured, smiling manner, Jack took the horn out of case and began playing softly without accompaniment. The musicians were transfixed. For hours Jack kept them awed, sitting there playing magnificent trombone solos.

Teagarden's style electrified the jazz world. He seemed to play effortlessly, almost lazily, the way he moved and spoke; but he could produce amazing triplets and runs and complicated phrases on an instrument that places great demands on the performer. But he never played just to show off mechanical skill. Every glissando, blue note and quick change of pace fitted into an over-all lovely, lyrical sense of theme. To the extent that he played with taste and restraint and was never rowdy or blatant, Teagarden was playing "cool" as far back as the twenties. He raised trombone solos to new heights as Coleman Hawkins was to do with the tenor saxophone in the early 1930's.

One of the stunts Teagarden often pulled was to remove the bell section of his trombone and play the slide directly into a drinking glass. This produced a pleasing, muted tone that he used to advantage on some of his blues numbers. The trombone normally comes apart between the slide and bell section so it can be fitted into a carrying case. Teagarden would simply take off the entire bell section which left him the slide and mouthpiece. He would hold the mouthpiece against his lips with his left hand while at the same time grasping the drinking glass near his cheek where the slide section, minus the bell, extended, covering this open end of the slide with the glass. The mouthpiece, glass and trombone were held in place with his left hand while he "ran his slide" with his right. More difficult than holding the instrument in this manner, the slide positions were altered, making playing more complex.

Teagarden sang the blues in his husky, drawling Texas baritone as naturally as he played them on his horn. Like Louis Armstrong, he possessed the ability to sing the same kind of jazz and blues licks that he played. He was at his plaintive best on "Basin Street Blues" and "I Got a Right To Sing the Blues."

He played with many famous bands including Ben Pollack's and Paul Whiteman's. At one time he led his own swing band. In 1947, he joined Louis Armstrong's All-Stars, a casual group of the greatest jazz luminaries ever assembled, including Earl "Fatha" Hines on piano, "Big Sid" Catlett on drums, Barney Bigard on clarinet, Arvell Shaw on bass and Satchmo leading the band. Teagarden remained with this bunch of jazz geniuses for four years then formed his own group and successfully toured Europe. This was followed in late 1958 by a tour of the Far East subsidized by the State Department.

During his career, Teagarden won much critical acclaim and many awards. His tall, big-shouldered figure, rugged features reflecting a mixture of German and Indian ancestry, thatch of black hair and slow grin were a familiar sight on the jazz scene until his sudden death in New Orleans in 1964.

Early in his career, Jack formed a lasting friendship and attachment for Louis Armstrong. The two made some of the top jazz recordings in history. The amusing duet they sing on the recording of "Rockin' Chair" is a jazz classic. Louis Armstrong is quoted in *Life* as saying when Jack passed from the scene:

> ". . . we understood each other so wonderful. There ain't going to be another Jack Teagarden. . . . He kept all his sad moments, his grievances to himself. But I could tell his whole heart, his life coming out of that horn. And it was all good."

The blues that Bessie Smith sang so eloquently, Jack Teagarden and Louis Armstrong played so movingly and Duke Ellington arranges so dramatically have given jazz its soul.

CHAPTER 17

BOP AND BEYOND

Service men returning to the States after World War II found the big-band era fading away, and they heard a strange new sound in music. A jazz revolution was taking place. It was as if a younger generation of jazz musicians had started talking in a new musical tongue. The new language was called bop.

Jazz had undergone changes before, from traditional New Orleans jazz to Dixieland to Chicago style to swing. In the past, each new style seemed to evolve naturally from that preceding it; but bop was a radical departure from the mainstream of jazz. It made a sharp break with many jazz traditions.

Jazz musicians and jazz fans are inclined to become emotional about their music. The dissension in the ranks over bop was loud and bitter. Many of the older, long-established musicians not only couldn't, or wouldn't, play bop, they hated it. In an article in *Down Beat,* Louis Armstrong called bop "that modern malice," and he made a recording that took a satirical dig at the new sound. Cab Calloway called bop "Chinese music." He warned Dizzy Gillespie, who was in his band, not to play bop. (The two eventually got in a fist fight and Gillespie parted company with the band to form his own group.) The younger musicians, going to the opposite extreme, sneered at all earlier forms of jazz. To the enthusiastic, young bop musicians, artists like Goodman or Armstrong were corny, square and hopelessly dated.

Just what was this new musical bombshell and how did it get started? It was the brainchild of a group of musical experimenters led by pianist Thelonious Monk, trumpeter Dizzy Gillespie, saxophonist Charlie Parker, drummer Kenny Clarke, arranger and pianist Mary Lou Williams and guitarist Charlie Christian.

There have always been special bars or after-hour places where musicians like to gather for jam sessions and to work out musical ideas. Such a place was a cabaret in Harlem called Minton's Playhouse. It was owned by Henry Minton, an old-time saxophone player and ex-musicians' union official. There was nothing unusual about the place—it was rather small and crowded, but there was a bandstand in the back room and musicians liked to congregate there for jam sessions. In the early forties it was one of the best places to go to hear top jazzmen.

One of the drawbacks of holding a jam session in a public place is there is no way to keep less talented musicians from horning in. Everyone wants to have his say. It "bugged" some of the more skillful musicians to be playing along smoothly, working out advanced ideas among themselves, and then to have things disrupted by an inept musician who walked up to the bandstand and joined in, spoiling the mood with his poor playing. So, a few of the regulars at Minton's figured out a way of discouraging the less adept. In *Hear Me Talkin To Ya* Dizzy Gillespie describes what happened:

> "No one man or group of men started modern jazz, but one of the ways it happened was this: Some

> of us began to jam at Minton's in Harlem in the early forties. But there were always some cats showing up there who couldn't blow at all but would take six or seven choruses to prove it.
>
> "So, on afternoons before a session, Thelonious Monk and I began to work out some complex variations on chords and the like, and we used them at night to scare away the no-talent guys.
>
> "After a while, we got more and more interested in what we were doing as music, and, as we began to explore more and more, our music evolved."

This new way of playing came to depend increasingly upon the performer's technical skill and upon an intellectual, rather than an emotional, approach to music.

While other musicians agree that Dizzy Gillespie decribed the situation at Minton's accurately, this is really an oversimplification of how modern jazz began. The truth is, pioneers were laying the groundwork for modern jazz as far back as the 1920's. For example, even though Bix played hot, Chicago-style jazz, he was searching for something beyond this—far ahead of his time. In the way-out chords of his piano compositions, in his preoccupation with serious modern composers such as Debussy and Stravinsky, in his interest in such a modern concept as the whole-tone scale and in the element of restraint in his cornet solos, the beginnings of new, intellectual ideas about jazz can be detected. His sidekick Frankie Trumbauer, another pioneer, played his C-melody sax with a light, airy tone that is emulated by some of today's cool sax men.

In the early 1930's, a new giant of jazz made an impact on the musical scene. His name was Coleman Hawkins, and he remains the undisputed master of the tenor saxophone. He gave the instrument a new concept of jazz expression, and since then all tenor-sax music has flowed directly, or indirectly, from Hawkins' inspiration.

Born in St. Joseph, Missouri, in 1904, Hawkins began playing jazz professionally at the age of fifteen in the band that accompanied blues singer Mamie Smith—not to be confused with Bessie. (It is interesting to note that Armstrong, Teagarden, Hines and Coleman Hawkins, outstanding innovators of their individual jazz instruments, were all launched on their professional careers by their mid-teens.) Hawkins came to New York with Mamie Smith, and then joined Fletcher Henderson's orchestra. He remained with Henderson until 1934 when he departed for Europe to carry on a successful jazz career overseas until his return to the United States in 1939.

Long before he left for Europe, Coleman Hawkins had become so famous that the tenor-sax men of the decade were trying to play like him. At that time Hawkins played with a full, rich, rather heavy tone, and it was this sound other tenor men strove to duplicate. Hawkins' classic recording was "Body and Soul," and one can only guess at the number of records other saxophone players wore out, copying this jazz gem, note for note. As a commentary on this man's genius, it can be pointed out that Hawkins' style has not remained static. It has changed with the times. The "Hawk" (also called "Bean") has kept abreast of new ideas and has become as modern and progressive as any sax man around.

However a tenor saxophonist who departed rather radically from the Hawkins style had more influence on the bop musicians who directly followed. Lester Young was born in Woodville, Mississippi, in 1909, and raised in New Orleans. His father was a bandleader on the Mississippi riverboats, and Lester played in his father's bands when still a youngster. He began on drums, found them too heavy to carry around, and took up the saxophone. He was one of the musicians who found employment in Kansas

City during the depression. He came to New York as soloist with Count Basie's band in 1936 and remained with the Count until 1940 when he formed his own band. Since then, he has played with various outstanding groups.

Young's playing made an impact on jazz musicians when he first appeared in New York. Anyone who had the audacity to play the tenor differently from Coleman Hawkins was worth listening to, and many young musicians around Harlem learned from Lester Young. His tone was small compared to the Hawk, and he used much less vibrato. His playing was cooler—that is, more restrained and objective, and he had a great feeling for the blues.

Just as Lester Young had departed from the accepted way of playing the tenor sax, a trumpet man of the 1930's had the originality to go off on a tangent from the Louis Armstrong style. He was David Roy Eldridge, sometimes called "Little Jazz." Like many leading Negro musicians of the swing era, he started with Fletcher Henderson's band, then formed his own small group in the late 1930's. After this he played with Gene Krupa, Artie Shaw and Benny Goodman, and toured with the Jazz at the Philharmonic group. Eldridge had considerable instrumental technique, and to form a style different from Armstrong, he would play solos that contained furious bursts of rapid runs and phrases. This new idea of fast fingering and a profusion of notes unquestionably influenced the young, up-and-coming, trumpet men, especially Dizzy Gillespie, who apparently decided that trumpet players had been sticking to the Armstrong tradition long enough, and it was time to venture toward new jazz frontiers.

So it can be said that Bix and Trumbauer, Lester Young and Roy Eldridge were among the principal pioneers along new paths of jazz expression that were to lead to bop and all the forms of cool and modern jazz that followed.

Certainly among the ranks of pioneer progressive jazzmen should be listed bandleader Stan Kenton. We are inclined to think of modern jazz as belonging to the 1950's and 1960's, but Kenton was playing progressive jazz in the 1940's. Kenton, a pianist, was better known as a composer and arranger. Born in Wichita, Kansas, in 1912, he studied under various teachers and wrote his first arrangement in 1928. It was toward the end of the swing era, in the early 1940's, that Kenton's large band burst on the musical scene with its new sound of dissonant harmonies. His 1943 recording of his theme "Artistry in Rhythm" was his most popular and best-known record of that period. Some of Kenton's ambitious concert work went so far afield of jazz it might better be classified as modern classical music. However, he also employed such gifted arrangers as Shorty Rogers, Gerry Mulligan and Bill Holman; and when playing their orchestrations, his band could swing in the old jazz tradition while experimenting with new harmonies and voicing. Kenton did not play bop, but he was a leader in the new sounds that came to jazz in the 1940's.

The new kind of jazz that Dizzy Gillespie and his buddies began playing at Minton's was called rebop, then bebop and finally just bop. One can find a dozen derivations of term, but no one really knows its origin. Musicians have a way of improvising on the English language as they do on musical themes. A new term was needed to describe this music and there it was—bop. It might have come from a meaningless phrase that a scat singer once uttered, or it could have had a relationship to some of the sounds of the new jazz licks.

Until bop came along, the strongest trademark of jazz and blues had been the beat, whether two or four strong beats to the measure. In bop, the steady boom-boom of the bass drum was conspicuous by its absence. The beat was implied more than stated by a soft swish-swish on the drummer's cymbals and by the four-beat rhythm of the stringed bass. The bass drum was reserved for explosive punctuation from time to time. This seeming lack of beat was more than disconcerting, it was detestable to many of the older jazz musicians who were accustomed to a strong 2/4 or 4/4 rhythmic foundation. Benny Goodman said there were two kinds of jazz, good and bad; and when you started messing up the beat, it was bad. An incident that occurred at Eddie Condon's nightclub illustrates a hot jazz musician's opinion of this new music. A waiter accidentally dropped a tray of dishes with an ear-shattering crash. Condon, a rhythmic guitarist and devotee of the Chicago and Dixieland schools of hot jazz, stopped his band, pointed an accusing finger at the guilty waiter and shouted, "We don't allow any of that progressive jazz in here!"

The bop enthusiasts, on the other hand, claimed there was a precedent for their ideas about rhythm which went all the way back to Africa. They pointed out that authentic African drumbeats were polyrhythmic—that is, several different rhythms going at the same time. By doing away with the restrictions of the overriding, steady two or four drumbeats to the measure, the bop soloist had more freedom to experiment with polyrhythms.

The bopsters also got away from the simpler melodic, lyrical idea of earlier jazz solos. Bop solos sound infinitely more complicated, almost like finger exercises from a book on advanced technique. Bop is played from the mind rather than the heart. The bop musician experiments with advanced ideas about harmony, exploring the sounds of chord alterations, chord substitutes and chord suspensions.

Each of the jazz eras had its leaders and heroes. If the followers of bop build a shrine it will no doubt be to trumpeter Dizzy Gillespie and alto saxophonist Charlie

Parker, nicknamed "Yardbird" or "Bird." In many respects, Charlie Parker's life parallels that of Bix. Both were experimenting with new ideas in jazz. Both were idols of their musical followers; both lived fast, dissipated lives; both died tragically young and quickly became legendary figures in the jazz world.

However, although the facts of Bix's life are pretty well known, there are elements of mystery and confusion about Parker. For example he died under rather unusual circumstances. In March, 1955, he was on his way to Boston to play a musical engagement, but stopped off first at the New York apartment of a friend, a wealthy and titled woman. While there, Parker was seized with a coughing spell so serious that a physician was summoned. Parker was ill three days, but by the evening of March 12th was feeling better. The doctor stopped by and said he was much improved. A half-hour later, while propped up in an armchair quietly watching television, Charlie Parker died. The exact cause of his death is still debated. His hostess said the doctor diagnosed Parker's illness as ulcers and cirrhosis of the liver. Newspaper stories attributed his death to pneumonia and a heart attack. Most likely the truth is that, as in Bix's case, his body was in such a weakened state that he quickly succumbed to an illness that someone in ordinary health would have survived.

Charlie Parker was not quite thirty-five when he died. Although even his exact birthdate is in doubt, August 29, 1920 is the generally accepted date. Kansas City, Kansas, was his home town. When he was about eleven, his mother bought him an alto saxophone. Aside from playing in the high-school band, he had little formal musical training. Parker quit school when he was fifteen and began running around with a bad crowd. He became addicted to narcotics when still a teen-ager, a curse that was to add much misery to his short and hectic life.

In the beginning Parker gave little indication that he was going to set the jazz world on fire. He had some humiliating experiences that could easily have caused him to give up music. According to one story, he tried to play in a jam session with Count Basie's band and performed so badly that drummer Jo Jones threw his cymbal across the room in disgust. On another occasion, he attempted a jazz chorus of "Body and Soul" at a night spot called the High Hat Club. Everyone laughed at him and he didn't touch his horn again for months.

But he returned to music and began playing professionally with the Jay McShann band in Kansas City in 1937. Most of his life Charlie Parker was a wanderer. According to one story, he drifted into New York around the end of 1938, so broke he didn't even have a horn. He went to work as a dishwasher in a Harlem after-hours club for nine dollars a week. Eight months went by before somebody finally gave him a horn and he began playing again. Whether these facts are strictly accurate or not, it is true that Parker was in New York in the early 1940's, that he met Dizzy Gillespie and teamed up with him and the bunch at Minton's and began his skyrocket flight to fame on the alto saxophone. He worked intermittently with several bands including Earl Hines', Cootie Williams', Andy Kirk's and Billy Eckstine's, though he usually played with four- and five-piece combos.

In trying to separate fact from fiction about Charlie Parker, one thing is certain: he led a tragic life. He went through cycles of illness, and when he was sick he played badly. But there were many times when he played brilliantly. He struggled with drug addiction all his life. The expensive habit kept him constantly broke. At times he tried to kick the habit only to turn to heavy drinking as a substitute. Some think the hostility of jazz musicians and critics to his new ideas of music drove him to retreat even more into narcotics and alcohol.

Late in 1945 while on a California tour with Dizzy Gillespie, he had a complete breakdown, and was committed to Camarillo State Mental Hospital where he spent six months. However, when he was released, he was once again playing and recording brilliantly. In the late 1940's, he made tours with Norman Granz's Jazz at the Philharmonic group, and in 1949, made a trip overseas to play at the Paris Jazz Festival. The last five years of his life were clouded with worsening emotional and physical problems, and he performed irregularly. A few months before his death he played one of his most brilliant concerts at Town Hall in New York City. On March 4, 1955, he put in a brief appearance at Birdland, the Manhattan nightclub named for him. It is said he played that night but quickly left the stand. A week later he was dead. When Dizzy Gillespie heard the news, he wept.

Unquestionably, Charlie Parker made a tremendous impact on modern jazz music. Jazz saxophonists from 1940 on, playing in a modern style, borrowed from Charlie Parker whether or not they realized it. Fundamentally Parker played the blues, and almost everything he played had blues roots and overtones. But he went far beyond the simple blues sounds of his predecessors. His improvisations were much more complex. When he first appeared on the music scene, many of his advanced harmonic ideas were strange, even unpleasant, to ears not accustomed to these sounds. Now after twenty years of exposure to modern jazz, when we go back and play the Bird's records they make sense to our ears.

Parker could play with fantastic drive, using a tone that was searing and bright, at times harshly angry. He played with tormented intensity much of the time, but he could be melodious. Rhythmically, Parker took liberties with the beat, giving his jazz choruses more subtle and varied punctuation, sudden bursts of notes that exploded in unexpected rebellion to the established tempo.

Because of all the experiments and liberties taken by the soloists with rhythm and harmony, bop was pretty much limited to small groups. These combos usually consisted of the soloist and a rhythm section that fed brief chord punctuations here and there. Some critics of this form of jazz point out that the long, involved solos could become monotonous.

Charlie Parker's illustrious colleague Dizzy Gillespie led a happier personal life than his friend. He was born in Cheraw, South Carolina, in 1917, and studied harmony and theory at the Laurinburg Institute in North Carolina. A happy-go-lucky individual, Gillespie clowned a lot, perhaps partly as a defense against criticism of his music. Bandleaders for whom he worked in the early 1940's were never sure if he was serious or just having fun with his far-out musical ideas.

On one occasion, somebody tripped over his horn, bending it out of shape. The result was an odd-shaped trumpet with the bell pointed upwards. Gillespie blew it, decided he liked it better because he could hear his own notes more clearly, and tried to have the design patented; but he found it had already been thought of. His crazy-shaped trumpet, his style of blowing with his cheeks swollen out like balloons, his mode of dress which included a beret, horn-rimmed glasses and a goatee were copied by many of his worshippers and created the stereotyped image of the bop musician of the 1940's.

But despite his eccentricities, Gillespie was universally respected as a jazzman. Even Louis Armstrong, who publically has never had a charitable word for bop, has praised Gillespie as a fine musician. In 1956, a band headed by Dizzy Gillespie toured Pakistan, Lebanon, Syria, Turkey, Yugoslavia and Greece, subsidized by the United States State Department. This was the first time the U. S. government paid official recognition to jazz and gave it economic aid. The success of this tour led to many more government sponsored foreign tours by other jazz groups.

The bop movement was at its peak from 1945 to 1950. Some big bands were quick to experiment with these new ideas, incorporating them in their arrangements and employing bop soloists. Woody Herman, Earl Hines and Billy Eckstine led the most important big bands to play bop.

However, bop limited itself by its very nature. Because the technical demands were so great, there were only a handful of musicians who could really master it. The majority of young jazzmen around the country had no ideas of their own to contribute and simply copied Parker and Gillespie, playing their notes over and over until they became stale clichés. The trademark of bop was a heavy use of the flatted fifth note. This flatted fifth became a cliché in itself. There was little in the music that the average listener could go home whistling, and the lack of a firm beat ruled it out as dance music. The simple fact is it was over most people's heads. And even some who understood it didn't particularly like it.

By the late 1940's, bop was a fad that was losing favor with audiences and musicians alike; and bop musicians were changing their pace. Dizzy Gillespie emphasized his singing and, like Armstrong, leaned more toward the role of entertainer while still doing superb trumpet work. Charlie Parker, in the last years of his life, made some recordings of old popular melodies, backed by a string section.

But the modern jazz movement was far from dead; a young trumpet player named Miles Davis, an admirer of Dizzy Gillespie, began recording in a style that reflected Gillespie's influence but a different mood. Where Gillespie had blown hot and wild, Davis blew in an introverted, dispassionate manner. His recordings made with a group playing arrangements by Gerry Mulligan, John Lewis and Gil Evans were the start of the era of cool jazz. These recordings were soon followed by other groups identified with the new, cool school of jazz and led by soloists like Stan Getz on tenor sax, Bobby Brookmeyer on trombone and Paul Desmond playing alto sax.

One thing bop accomplished was to bring jazz back from the big, heavily arranged bands to smaller groups with more room for personal expression. Cool jazz returned to the old Dixieland idea of small groups playing in counterpoint. However, there was a great deal of difference between cool jazz and Dixieland, especially in rhythm. In Dixieland and Chicago-style hot jazz, the musicians crowded or pushed ahead of the beat, creating an urgent, frenetic effect. The swing musicians achieved a more relaxed mood by staying on beat. The cool jazz players produced an even more relaxed style by lagging somewhat behind the beat. Cool musicians strive for a light and dry tone, usually with very little vibrato. The main characteristics of cool jazz are understatement and restraint. The hot jazz musician played with great feeling and emotion while the devoted cool jazzman played with intellectual detachment.

The new order of the day became, "Be cool, man." That meant to perform with an air of aloof dignity, of studied nonchalance, and never, *never* "sell out"—a jazz slang expression meaning to clown or use exaggerated effects to please the audience. If one ventures to read a social meaning into the idea of "cool" in respect to the

Negro, he might suggest that these young musicians were rebelling against the slap-happy, ingratiating, Uncle Tom image that white society had placed on the colored entertainer since the days of the minstrels.

The young audience of the swing bands of the 1930's had been the jitterbuggers. In 1950, they became the hipsters, a word derived from "hip" which had been "hep" in the swing days (in the 1960's the word was modified again to fit an entirely different kind of young crowd the "hippies"). The hipster of the 1950's, who dug his jazz sounds with the same air of intellectual dispassion as the cool musicians, "put down" the older musicians of the swing and hot-jazz eras. For many of them, jazz music was invented by Dizzy Gillespie and Charlie Parker. The cool assurance of some of these extremists was just a pose and they had little idea of what was going on musically. Unfortunately, in some cases, neither did the musicians!

But there were plenty of musicians playing new forms of jazz who knew very well what was going on. These included the West Coast groups headed by trumpeter Shorty Rogers and saxophonist Gerry Mulligan. There were new pianists. George Shearing from England headed a quintet that played its own brand of smooth, modified bop. Oscar Peterson came down from Canada swinging in the modern vein and Erroll Garner played a style all his own.

The West Coast pianist to make the biggest impact, especially with college audiences, was Dave Brubeck. Brubeck had majored in music at college and studied under such serious composers as Darius Milhaud and Arnold Schoenburg, then served in World War II. He launched his career as a jazz musician when he became a civilian again. First appearing in San Francisco, he caused quite a stir in jazz circles; quickly his piano style and modern jazz combo became nationally known. His quartet toured the nation making concert and nightclub appearances. They were on the program at the Newport [Rhode Island] Jazz Festival in 1958 and following this enjoyed a highly successful tour of Europe.

Brubeck's piano style is complex harmonically, no doubt because of his interest in modern classical composition. He experiments with rhythms that are unconventional in jazz, such as the jazz waltz.

One either likes Brubeck a great deal, or not at all. A jazz fan who prefers the simpler, more understandable jazz of a less sophisticated era will find Brubeck boring. On the other hand if the listener is interested in new jazz vistas, in the application of modern compositional concepts to the jazz keyboard, if he likes his jazz cool and cerebral, he may become a devoted Brubeck follower. Although Brubeck rose to fame in the 1950's, he remains one of the top figures in the jazz field today.

Brubeck is representative of a trend among jazz musicians of the 1950's and 1960's to be college trained and to have a serious, professional attitude toward their art. This academic background has led to greater melodic, harmonic and rhythmic complexities in jazz. More and more elements of classical music have been absorbed. The Modern Jazz Quartet is particularly representative of this trend. Founded by the brilliant pianist John Lewis, the Quartet relies heavily on written scores in which an almost classical style of counterpoint predominates. Their approach is soft, gentle and oblique. While some critics question that they play jazz at all, they have risen to international prominence and have won many polls and awards, as well as much popular acclaim.

The search for new sounds and ideas brought new instruments into jazz groups in the 1950's. An increasing interest in Afro-Cuban and Latin American rhythms resulted in popularity of exotic drums: bongos, Conga drums and timbals. The flute, rarely associated with jazz in earlier periods, is now often heard. The French horn and oboe, normally used in symphonic orchestras, found their way into the hands of some jazz performers. There is even a jazz bagpipe player around!

The latest development in jazz is the New Wave or the New Thing. In 1959, a young saxophonist named Ornette Coleman appeared on the scene making strange sounds with a white, plastic, alto saxophone. His music was so radical that some angry jazz fans wanted to chase him off the bandstand. Critics, trying to find something kind to say, ventured that at least Coleman was an innovator. Not one to be put down easily, Coleman has stuck around and has a small but intense group of followers among musicians who skirt the brink of starvation while refusing to sell themselves by playing commercially acceptable jazz. What they do play has been described by some as utter chaos and by others as abstract jazz, the musical counterpart of abstract painting.

The New Thing does away with almost all musical disciplines and restrictions. There are no harmonic chord progressions to follow; the performer plays anything that comes to mind in a totally uninhibited method of expression. The music is atonal, which is to say that no musical scale or key is followed. Anything goes. There is no set rhythmic pattern.

Besides Ornette Coleman, some other jazzmen associated with the New Thing are Don Ellis (trumpet), Sunny Murray (drums), Marion Brown (alto sax), Don Cherry (trumpet), Jimmy Giuffre (trumpet), Bill Dixon (trumpet) and Albert Ayler (tenor sax).

Some critics say this kind of musical expression goes back to the field cry and earliest blues which were more human cries of anguish or happiness than music. The lack of discipline in art can be invigorating. It can also lead to abuse. But it is too early to say where the New Thing will lead, whether anything lasting in jazz will come of it, or if it is good in itself. It is easy to criticize this experiment. The sounds grate on ears unaccustomed to atonality. Some of the solos seem interminable, frequently lasting as long as an hour. But there was a time when music critics described Dixieland jazz as nothing but a collection of barnyard squawks and hollers, and said it could not be dignified by calling it music.

One thing is certain. A lively art like jazz is in a constant state of evolution and full of surprises for listener and performer alike. Who knows what next year will bring?

CHAPTER 18

POPULAR TRENDS

Jazz floating across the river from a steamboat paddling down the Mississippi . . . a piano player in a Storyville honky-tonk . . . blues in the night . . . the noise of machine guns in a Chicago gang war . . . one-night stands . . . a hot clarinet . . . a cool tenor sax . . . a Duke Ellington arrangement . . . a jam session in a basement in the early dawn hours—all these are colorful fragments of the passing parade of jazz. And they bring us to the music of today.

The American bandmaster John Philip Sousa, "the March King," is supposed to have remarked that jazz music would endure as long as people heard it through their feet and not their heads. In the past, people did just that. One might prefer to sit and listen, but the rhythm was there for dancing. The New Orleans bands of Buddy Bolden's time, the Austin High boys who played in Chicago speakeasies and the swing bands of the thirties played music that people danced to.

Then, beginning in the late 1940's, people began doing what Mr. Sousa warned against; they began listening to jazz with their heads instead of their feet. The sophisticated forms of progressive jazz—bop and cool—got away from the beat and appealed mainly to the intellect, thus losing the dance audiences and limiting their following to a small segment of the avant-garde. Modern jazz styles put greater demands on the performer and at the same time on the listener. One needs considerable knowledge of harmony and theory to understand fully a progressive jazz solo. Furthermore, the dissonant harmonies are punctuated by nervous, complicated rhythms that make dancing almost impossible.

Despite Mr. Sousa's dire prediction, the new jazz has endured and has an enthusiastic audience. But it is no longer dance music and a widening gulf has separated it from what we call popular music.

By the mid 1950's, the restless young people, seeking earthier, rhythmic music, had turned away from the no-beat sound of cool jazz and bop, to the all-beat sound of a very primitive jazz rhythm—the country blues of the deep South. These were the blues that Blind Lemon Jefferson and Leadbelly played and sang. But there was a new addition. Since the 1930's, the soul music of the cotton-field shanties and gospel churches had been given a hard-driving beat by some performers, and the new combination of blues and beat was called "rhythm and blues." It was played by Negro performers for Negro audiences. Some of the top rhythm and blues artists were Chuck Berry, Bo Diddley, Muddy Waters and John Lee Hooker. Their music was recorded on race records, and for a while the white audiences knew nothing about them.

In 1951 a disc jockey in Cleveland named Alan Freed put the name "rock 'n' roll" to this kind of rhythm and blues and began to play it for a general audience. He was a fast-talking, hard-selling deejay who sometimes sang along with the records and whammed a telephone book to the beat. Freed launched a new form of American popular music.

It would have been technically impossible for rock 'n' roll to have happened in the twenties or thirties, at least in the form we know it, simply because the equipment was not then available. Rock 'n' roll is a musical phenomenon of the electronic age. It depends upon powerful hi-fi amplifiers that can drown the senses in an all-powerful beat. The southern rhythm and blues performers began to use the electric guitar, electric bass and microphones when they migrated to the industrial North after World War II. The beat became the big beat, more powerful, dominating the melody and nearly drowning the singer's words.

Bill Haley was one of the first recording artists to come up with hit rock 'n' roll recordings. His "Crazy Man Crazy," recorded in 1951, eventually sold a million copies. In 1953, he recorded "Rock around the Clock" another big moneymaker.

But it was up to a youngster from Tennessee to become the first, and perhaps the greatest, hero of the rock 'n' roll age. His name was Elvis Presley. Sporting three-inch sideburns, a deadpan expression and singing in a husky hillbilly accent while gyrating his hips, he made his national debut on the Jimmy and Tommy Dorsey television show in the fall of 1956. At once be became a howling success with a nationwide and soon a worldwide teen-age following. He made hits of songs like "Don't Step on My Blue Suede Shoes" and "You Ain't Nothin' But a Hound Dog." Elvis soon had adolescents screaming and fainting on the same grand scale as their mothers had done a generation earlier over Frank Sinatra. But where Frankie wore suits and sang ballads in a respectable manner, Elvis seemed to sing with a kind of sneer aimed at adult authority. His movements were called obscene by adults who viewed him with a mixture of alarm and distaste. And thereby rested the secret of his popularity with the young people. He was an extension of the James Dean legend, personifying teen-age rebellion against the restricting adult world.

Self-proclaimed moralists were indignant over Elvis, and he became the target of music critics as well. Clergymen were alarmed over his effect on teen-age morality. When he appeared, riots were apt to occur. A Senate subcommittee investigated a possible link between juvenile delinquency and rock 'n' roll. Adults and devotees of more refined music wistfully hoped they'd wake up one morning and Elvis would be gone. "He can't last," they reassured each other. "He's just a fad."

One day in 1958 he was gone—drafted into the army. "Well, that's the end of *him,*" any number of parents sighed. But Elvis' popularity proved indestructible. His fans remained loyal during his army years and when he reappeared in civilian life, a superannuated teen-ager, he found Hollywood waiting for him with open arms. He regularly turns out one or two movies a year; and bad or good, his pictures consistently have large box-office returns. Elvis, it is estimated, grosses two million dollars a year from movies, records and assorted items bearing his name, such as Elvis Presley T-shirts.

Despite his early image as the world's foremost juvenile delinquent, the rather surprising fact is that Elvis doesn't drink, smoke or swear. He is very polite, and was a model soldier. In Hollywood he shies away from nightclubs and has little to do with the social life of the movie crowd, preferring to stay with a close circle of buddies and business associates from Tennessee who accompany him wherever he goes. The critics and adults who once reviled him have grown rather fond of Elvis, now past thirty. He didn't turn out to be such a villain after all.

But back in the late 1950's when much of the adult population viewed rock 'n' roll in much the same category as an Asian flu epidemic, unpleasant but bound to pass, a scandal broke that could have been the death blow to the big beat. It appeared that certain record companies were bribing selected disc jockeys to plug specific rock 'n' roll releases over the air. This unethical and illegal practice was called "payola."

"Because of this," analyzed the adults, "the rock 'n' roll fad is dead. Now maybe we can turn on the radio and hear tunes like 'Stardust' again."

Far from it. The very next year, 1960, a tubby entertainer named Chubby Checker was launched on the rock 'n' roll scene. "Let's do the Twist, baby," he invited everyone. And at the Peppermint Lounge in Manhattan, the dance crowd took up his invitation and suddenly teenagers across the nation stopped doing the worn-out jitterbug. They now had a dance all their own.

The Twist was simple enough. The dancers faced one another, planted their feet firmly, and went into an arm-swinging, hip-rotating movement as if drying their backs with towels. Adults continued to say hopefully, though with less and less conviction, "Well, rock 'n' roll is just a passing fad," while they, themselves did the Twist at the country club on Saturday nights.

Then England appeared on the scene, launching an invasion some declared was a long-delayed counterattack to our Revolution of 1776. The British force consisted of four young rock'n'roll-ers who stepped off the plane wearing tight, Edwardian suits, high-heeled boots and hair down to their eyes. They were promptly mobbed by screaming, fainting adolescent girls. They called themselves the Beatles and they won an instant victory in America, as they already had in England and Europe.

When they appeared on the "Ed Sullivan Show" in

February of 1964, they drew one of the largest audiences in television history. They proved to be charming and refreshing and firmly established themselves as leaders on the rock 'n' roll scene. Their music was based on the rhythm and blues concept, but they put a new, light-hearted touch to the previously heavier blues mood. In the year 1964 alone, the Beatles earned some fourteen million dollars and made the barber shop a place to be avoided by teen-agers the world over. They have written some very lovely songs including "Yesterday" and "Michelle," in addition to appearing in two successful films.

The Beatles were followed by another highly popular English group, the Rolling Stones. These two groups, and many of their countrymen have done something rather remarkable. They made London into a world center of fads in dress and popular music. Mod fashions and the Mersey sound are big on the teen-age scene. In earlier years, America had been the world source for jazz and popular music. Now it has strong competition from London. Actually Liverpool, overlooking the Mersey River, is the pop-music capital of the British Isles and the city which gave birth to the Beatles and the Rolling Stones. The English hit parade is dominated by Mersey sound.

In America two new styles are big on the popular music scene. The "Motown sound" of Detroit is Negro inspired, big-city blues music with a driving beat, while California-style rock 'n' roll called "surf sound," is personified by the Beach Boys, who produce a light, staccato beat and sing about California teen-age pastimes—surfing and cars.

Singing groups and styles are a difficult subject to write about. They change so rapidly, from one day to the next, that anything we could say about the subject here would be dated before our book could be printed. Some personalities, however, have made such outstanding hits that they are bound to leave a lasting impression on the popular-music scene. For example, there is the female singing group the Supremes. These three Negro girls grew up together in a squalid housing project in Detroit to become the reigning princesses of the rock 'n' roll world. Ray Charles is also in a class by himself as a singer, pianist and bandleader. Charles is essentially a blues singer, one of the finest, and he probably comes the closest to producing lasting jazz art based on the driving rock beat.

Herman's Hermits, Paul Revere and the Raiders, the Animals—the list could go on and on; each group has its particular gimmick of sound and dress that catches the fickle teen-age imagination for a while but often are as quickly forgotten.

More important to a study of jazz and popular music than the groups who come and go is the music itself. Why has rock 'n' roll become the sound of the young generation from Liverpool to Tokyo? It's what's happening among young people the world over. It's the music of high-school proms, the music of the protesters, the hippies and the kids down the block. Folk singers and poets like Bob Dylan and Phil Ochs have come up with a hybrid style of "folk-rock" that combines folk singing and the rock 'n' roll beat to accompany their lyrics.

To begin with, rock 'n' roll is the music teen-agers identify with. It belongs to them. It's their music. In its heavy, driving, all-encompassing beat, they find an outlet for the frustrations and aggressions of a world that grows more complex and confining every day, a world where there are fewer and fewer outlets for teen-age energy and enthusiasm.

The dances that have developed around this music—the Watusi, the Frug, the Monkey, the Swim, the Boogaloo—are more energetic body movements than actual dance steps, a kind of primitive reflex response to the hypnotic, thundering beat. It is interesting to note that these dances have, for the first time, given a girl complete freedom on the dance floor. In all the previous dance styles, including the jitterbug, she was expected to follow her male partner's lead and domination. Now she dances apart, on her own, facing her partner, but unrestricted by him. Perhaps the rock dances are another symbol of the modern girl's declaration of freedom and equality.

As for rock 'n' roll itself, one could say it is music older than jazz. The history of jazz goes back some sixty or seventy years. The history of the steady, simple beat is as old as mankind. When the dancer loses himself completely in this throbbing pulse, his consciousness becomes blurred and he is hardly aware of the music. Rock 'n' roll has been criticized as being monotonous—but that is its purpose. It is not music to listen to, but music to move to. Rock 'n' roll is our modern version of rituals that have existed in other societies as far back as the time when primitive man shuffled and stomped around a drummer pounding on a hollow log until he fell in a state of mystic frenzy. The religious dances of the American Indian, African tribal dances, the pagan rituals of ancient civilizations and the dancing and shaking that accompanies worship in some Christian churches—these are all first cousins to the big beat of rock 'n' roll.

But we then arrive at the question—is rock 'n' roll jazz?

The most fundamental element of jazz—improvisation—is lacking in rock 'n' roll. When a jazzman improvises, he is making his own musical statement, his extemporaneous composition; and it must be carefully listened to. If one had to listen too closely to such creations in rock 'n' roll, the hypnotic effect of the beat would be lost. Furthermore, the heavy beat would have to become secondary to the jazz solo or the contrapuntal jazz inventions of the ensemble. And then it would no longer be rock 'n' roll, where *everything,* even the words of the vocalist, must be lost in the beat.

One could easily play jazz to a rock 'n' roll rhythm and some groups do, but are they playing rock 'n' roll? Not really.

It is always dangerous to make dogmatic statements about anything as full of surprises and changes as jazz. Perhaps in the future there will be some kind of blending between rock 'n' roll and jazz. For the present, we must hold to the view that jazz is jazz and rock 'n' roll is rock 'n' roll; and there is a difference.

The difference or separation between our current popular music and jazz has caused some pessimism among jazz fans. They lament that the days of fine, big-band jazz music are dead and gone, that the kids nowadays only want to hear rock 'n' roll. And yet Harry James, Woody Herman, Count Basie, Duke Ellington, Buddy Rich and many others are still leading highly successful big bands that enjoy steady bookings and big record sales; and these groups continue to play some of the finest jazz music ever heard.

There are others who have said the last rites over Dixieland and traditional New Orleans jazz, saying the older musicians are dying out and their style of playing is dying with them. And yet there has been a great revival of interest in Dixieland all over the nation. Hometown groups, many of them composed of men who are successful in other professions, keep the sound of two-beat jazz alive. On the West Coast, trombone player Turk Murphy leads a group of fundamentalists who consider anything newer than King Oliver "progressive." In San Antonio, Texas, Jim Cullen, a successful wholesale grocer, leads the Happy

Jazz Band—a group that makes "the good times roll" with their Dixie beat. Cullen's son plays cornet very much in the Bix Beiderbecke tradition. Then in Los Angeles there is the Firehouse Five, a sideline endeavor of artists who work at the Walt Disney studios by day. The Crawford-Ferguson Night Owls of New Orleans are composed of an airline representative who pounds the drums, a surgeon who whangs the banjo, a banker who thumps the bass and a Ph.D. who noodles on the clarinet. The Boll Weevil Jazz Band of Ann Arbor, Michigan, and the Easy Rider Jazz Band of Bridgeport, Connecticut, are only two of many such semi-professional, regional groups. Music may be only a sideline to these people, who all hold other full-time jobs, but it is obviously their true love, and they continually prove there is a steady audience for the older, traditional forms of jazz.

There are also many professional groups and individual jazz stars who successfully play "mainstream" jazz—that is, jazz that is neither old-fashioned nor highly progressive, but up-to-date in harmonies and rhythms and performed with a great degree of skill. Mainstream jazz keeps what is good from the past and blends it with a conservative appreciation of newer ideas; and its popularity on records and in booking dates indicates a receptive audience.

The truth is that jazz is enjoying a period of greater variety and more importance than ever before. One can listen to traditional, New Orleans jazz played in Preservation Hall in New Orleans by white-haired jazzmen who remember the street parades and the days of Storyville, or he can hear avant-garde, abstract jazz played by Ornette Coleman and all the styles in between.

Jazz music has always been closely linked with the record industry. When long-playing 33⅓ rpm records appeared in the late 1940's, to be swiftly followed by high fidelity and then stereo systems, one could hear jazz performances of high quality reproduced in his home. No longer is the jazz buff restricted to one melody on each side of a scratchy 78 rpm platter. Now he can listen to whole jazz concerts and jam sessions recorded on the spot and brought to him in long-playing record albums or on tape. The expanding market for jazz recordings is proof of an audience for this music.

And there are the jazz festivals, consistently drawing large crowds hungry for good jazz. The first of these took place at Newport, Rhode Island, in the summer of 1954. It was an open-air concert, attracting a number of leading jazz performers. So successful is this summer festival that activities expanded from two days to five by 1960, and additional festivals have been put on in other cities under the auspices of the Newport promoters. The Monterey Jazz Festival attracts top performers, as does the *Playboy Magazine* indoor festival at the Chicago Stadium, which in the summer of 1959, drew seventy thousand spectators. The annual jazz festival in Austin, Texas, is also highly successful and lists such outstanding jazz luminaries as Woody Herman's band, Coleman Hawkins and Pee Wee Russell.

There are many smaller, regional jazz festivals such as the one held each summer in Corpus Christi, Texas. There are no big jazz names here; the performers are drawn from local and regional areas, yet a capacity crowd always attends, proving once again that people are still hungry for the sound of jazz.

Yes, jazz music is very much alive and healthy, very much a part of what's happening. In the words of Louis Armstrong, "Listen to it, Pops. The whole world's turned on. Don't you dig its pretty sounds?"

BIBLIOGRAPHY

This bibliography lists books and articles from which, with the kind permission of the authors and publishers, I have quoted. I hope it will serve to stimulate further reading in the field. Also I would like to take this opportunity to thank Red Camp, the jazz pianist, for the many verbal jam sessions we had about this project.

CAMPBELL, MARY. "The Duke Wants No Vacation from Music," Associated Press feature, September, 1967.

CARMICHAEL, HOAGY. *The Stardust Road,* Rinehart, New York, N. Y. 1946. (out of print).

CONDON, EDDIE and SUGRUE, THOMAS. *We Called It Music,* Holt, New York, N. Y. 1947 (out of print).

FEATHER, LEONARD. *The Encyclopedia of Jazz, the new edition,* Horizon Press, 156 Fifth Avenue, New York, N. Y. 10010, 1960. $15.00.

KING, LARRY L. "Everybody's Louie," *Harper's Magazine,* November 1967.

MERYMAN, RICHARD. "An Interview with Louis Armstrong," *Life,* April 15, 1966.

MEZZROW, MEZZ and WOLF, BERNARD. *Really the Blues,* paperback edition New American Library, 1301 Avenue of the Americas, New York, N. Y. 10019. 1964. 75¢

PECK, IRA (ed.). *The New Sound, Yes!* The Four Winds Press, 50 West 44th Street, New York, N. Y. 10036. 1966.

SHAPIRO, NAT and HENTOFF, NAT (eds.). *Hear Me Talkin' to Ya,* paperback edition Dover Publications, 180 Varick Street, New York, N. Y. 10014. 1966. $2.00.

STEARNS, MARSHALL. *The Story of Jazz,* paperback edition New American Library, 1301 Avenue of the Americas, New York, N. Y. 10019, fourth printing 1964. 75¢. Hardcover edition Oxford University Press, $7.50.

ULANOV, BARRY. *A History of Jazz in America,* The Viking Press, 625 Madison Avenue, New York, N. Y. 10022. 1952. $5.00.

WALKER, LEO. *Great Dance Bands,* Howell-North Books, 1050 Parker Street, Berkeley, Calif. 94710. 1964. $10.00.